13 KEYS TO BUSINESS SUCCESS

Best Strategies For Business Success

BY PROPHET TAYO DEMOLA

Edited by Tadray Concept Publishers

Professional Book Editors & Publishers

Lagos, Nigeria

Bible Quotations: All Bible Quotations are taken from the New King James Version of the Holy Bible.

First Published May 2021 by Tadray Concept Publishers

Copyright © Prophet Tayo Demola May 2021

The literary rights of the author have been asserted.

All rights reserved.

No part of this publication may be reproduced or transmitted by any means, without formal prior written permission from the author.

Enquiries:
All enquiries should be directed to the Publishers:
Tadray Concept Publishers
Professional Book Editors & Publishers
Lagos, Nigeria
Tel: +2348039158449,
+2348039158449.
Email: professionaleditors47@gmail.com

CONTENTS

Dedication

Preface

CHAPTER 1

Good Product Or Service

Prayer To Stop Spiritual Pollution In Your Business
Scriptures For Meditation

CHAPTER 2

Consistent Promotions & Advertising
Prayer To Announce You To The World & For Upliftment In Your Business
Scriptures For Meditation

CHAPTER 3

Good Financial Investment In Promotions
Prayer For Financial Favor To Expand Your Business
Scriptures For Meditation

CHAPTER 4

Long Period Of Promotions
Prayer For Healing And Deliverance Over Your Life And Family
Scriptures For Meditation

CHAPTER 5

Having Multiple Products Or Services
Prayer Of Impartation To Receive Unique Business Ideas
Scriptures For Meditation

CHAPTER 6

Proper Business Branding
Tips For Proper Business Branding
Prayer For Supernatural Grace To Serve God In Your Business
Scriptures For Meditation

CHAPTER 7

Good Customer Service

Why Many Businesses Crash

Prayers To Cancel Past Mistakes That Want To Crash Your Business

Scriptures For Regular Reading For Business Success

Scriptures For Meditation

CHAPTER 8
Good Pricing System
Deliverance Prayers Against Greed And Covetousness
Scriptures For Meditation

CHAPTER 9
Studying Your Customers
Tips On Business & Customer Survey
Prayers For Supernatural Favor And Abundance
Scriptures For Meditation

CHAPTER 10
Running Promos & Giving Of Bonuses
Tips On Running Promos & Giving Freebies
Prayers To Bring Good Customers
Scriptures For Meditation

CHAPTER 11
Proper Communication With Your Customers
Tips On Sustaining Communication With Your Clients
Prayer For Financial Favor, Open Heavens And Financial Breakthrough In Your Business
Scriptures For Meditation

CHAPTER 12
Why Patience Is Vital
Prayers To Break Demonic Spells, Demonic Yokes And Demonic Curses Over Your Business & Finances
Scriptures For Meditation

CHAPTER 13

Why You Need A Social Media Manager

Strategies For Social Media Management

Responsibilities Of Social Media Manager

My Prayers For You Over Your Employees

Scriptures For Meditation

CHAPTER 14

Epilogue: Your Business Will Succeed

Deliverance & Breakthrough Prayers For Your Business

CHAPTER 15

What's Your Hope Of Eternity?

CHAPTER 16

25 Miraculous Psalms

CHAPTER 17

My Letter To Parents

Consultation, Counseling And Prayers

Partner With me

Kindly Drop A Review

About The Author

DEDICATION

To all business owners all over the world.

To all entrepreneurs all over the world.

The Lord will bless your business and lift you up beyond your imagination in Jesus name. Amen.

To all business minded people, wherever you are.

To every person who is struggling to make a living with their business.

The good Lord will never let you down in Jesus name. Amen.

The Lord will shower you with His infinite mercies and supernatural favor in Jesus name. Amen.

The Lord will bless you with financial breakthrough and financial abundance in Jesus name. Amen.

The peace of the Lord be with you in Jesus name. Amen.

PREFACE

Why is it that many businesses crash within a few years after establishing them?

Why do people lose a lot of money in business and still end up closing the business? Why is it so difficult for many people to run their businesses successfully?

Why are people so scared of starting their own businesses and instead prefer to work for others? What is the secret of business success that makes some succeed and others fail? Why are some businesses booming and expanding while others are closing shop?

This book delves into a lot of issues regarding business and how you can achieve success in your business. It was written to inspire you as a business owner to achieve success in your business.

This divinely inspired and anointed book has a lot of prayers at the end of each chapter. It also has scriptures for meditation at the end of each chapter.

In this book, you will find out why some businesses crash no matter how hard the business owner tried to protect it. There are spiritual mysteries that people do not know about businesses because the spiritual realm controls the physical realm. The crashing of a business is more spiritual than physical.

So this book reveals the secret of what holds many businesses captive and what crumbles businesses, so that entrepreneurs and business owners can be blessed with this revelation and work on their businesses to achieve success.

Just read and claim the prayers in faith and also meditate on the scriptures. The Lord will do it for you if you believe.

For there is nothing our God cannot do. For with man it is impossible, but with God all things are possible. (Matthew 19:26)

Believe it and you will achieve it.

Yours sincerely,
Prophet Tayo Demola
May 5th, 2021.

CHAPTER 1

GOOD PRODUCT OR SERVICE

"Do you see a man who excels in his work? He will stand before kings; He will not stand before unknown men." (Proverbs 22:29)

Do you know that a good product sells itself? Do you know that a bad product is a bad advertisement to the person or company that produced it?

Will you be happy after buying a product with your hard earned money and later discover that it's useless and can't serve the purpose for which you bought it? How would you feel after using it and you got disappointed?

You discovered that all the claims by the seller or manufacturer were actually untrue. You found out that they were mere gimmicks. They actually packaged the product to deceive the people into believing it's genuine whereas it's not. They made it look so real. They made it so enticing and believable but you later discovered it was a trap.

After using it, you now wished you never bought it in the first place. You now realised you've wasted your money. This kind of situation has happened to a lot of people. Sometimes these marketers and promoters can market and package a product so beautifully well but it's all a trap to take your money.

It can be very annoying to discover that a product you relied so much to solve your needs can disappoint you at the time you need it most. But guess what? The manufacturer has disappointed himself by producing a bad product.

A bad product is nothing but an advertisement of the negligence and incompetence of the manufacturer. It's simply an announcement by the manufacturer that people should stop patronizing him.

It is very certain that any manufacturer who continues to produce bad products will soon go out of business and would have to close shop. No doubt about it.

Your business is your source of income and it must matter so much to you. It is very important and you must take it seriously. What you sow into your business is what you will eventually reap.

So if you sow good seeds of diligence and excellence into your business then you will definitely reap good returns and bumper harvest. But if you sow the seeds of mediocrity and negligence, the results can be unpalatable.

Have you imagined why some companies have so many customers and no matter what they produce, people will buy? But there are others who try to package themselves so well, yet people hardly patronize them however hard they tried.

Have you thought of why some businesses grow so fast that within a short period of time people would have known them all over the country? Have you ever thought of what happened to some businesses you knew before but no one ever hears about them anymore?

If you bought a product from a company and later discovered it to be a bad product or it didn't serve the purpose for which it was sold, would you ever patronize such a company again, even if they have other products they produce? You are likely not to ever trust them again with your money. You won't even want to waste your money anymore.

So when people say a good product sells itself, this is really true. If the product is good, you will buy more of it next time. More people will buy it and even recommend it to others and gradually more people will begin to buy and recommend it. Then it will begin to sell to places the manufacturer did not advertise it. So a good product will advertise itself.

As a business owner, the cheapest way to advertise your products or services is to ensure you produce quality products and offer excellent services, no matter what it will cost you to do so.

If you are trying to economize your resources by producing cheap and substandard products, it will hurt your business in the long run because of the number of people who would have been turned away from patronizing you by your inferior products or services.

It will even give you peace of mind to know that you're offering your customers the best product or service which will serve them the value for their money. It's even better that your product or service serves a value that is far more than the cost of such a product. If you are able to achieve this, you will have a continuous demand for more of your products or services.

The business world is so complex and competitive all over the world. What you think you're doing well is what another person is doing even better than you. But there's no one who does not value quality products or services. This is what moves people to even be willing to pay more.

Are your customers satisfied? Can they confidentiality come back to look for your products on their own with money in their pockets and ready to buy even if you've increased the price? Are they willing to keep buying it despite your price increases?

What makes your business succeed is when your customers are happy with your product or services. Happy customers make great businesses. Sad customers ruin businesses and make them close shop.

Remember that without the customers your business is dead. Your business will only succeed if you have customer patronage and without having good products that will satisfy the needs of your customers they will not patronize you.

The book of Proverbs 22:29 talks about how a diligent man can be catapulted to meet with a king just because he has exhibited a certain level of excellence in his work. He has shown that he can be trusted. He has paid the price for honor and therefore he can now meet with the president because his excellent work or talent has made it possible for him.

His work has now been accepted into the hall of fame. Before now, he was displaying it before ordinary men, but because this kind of talent is too excellent to be hidden, he has now been catapulted to meet with the king or the president.

This is what diligence and excellence can bring. A careless, shabby and ignorant person cannot achieve this kind of thing. Only a hardworking person who sticks to excellence and quality without compromising his standards can achieve this.

So having a good product or service is very important if you're serious about growing your business and taking it to the next level.

May the Lord give you the grace for integrity, excellence, quality and speed in your business endeavors in Jesus name. Amen.

The peace of the Lord be with you in Jesus name. Amen.

PRAYER TO STOP SPIRITUAL POLLUTION IN YOUR BUSINESS

1. Any plot of the enemy to pollute or adulterate your products in the spiritual realm with fake products in order to embarrass you, in order to tarnish your image, in order to spoil your reputation and crash your business, by the authority in the Blood of Jesus Christ shed on the cross of Calvary, I cancel their evil plans right now in Jesus name. Amen.

2. Any plan of the enemy to incite people against you or against your business in order to cause trouble and crash your business, I destroy all their evil plans right now in Jesus name. Amen.

3. Any evil plan by the enemy to use people to fabricate falsehood against you and report you or your business to the authorities and cause the government to close down your business, I cancel it right now in Jesus name. Amen.

4. Any plot of the enemy to divert your customers away from you and make them not to patronize you, I destroy their evil plans right now in Jesus name. Amen.

5. Any human being or demonic agent that has vowed to be a stumbling block to your success, right now I destroy their evil powers by the power of the holy ghost and I command them and their demonic agents to die by fire in Jesus name. Amen.

6. Every demonic spirit that has been assigned to monitor your life and to cause promise and fail in your life and business, I destroy their powers right now and set you free in Jesus name. Amen.

7. Every demonic spirit that has been assigned to you to cause near success syndrome in your life, by the authority in the Blood of Jesus Christ, I destroy their powers right now in Jesus name. Amen.

8. Any agent of darkness that has been sent to wait for you at the point of your success to cause trouble for you in order to make you lose your success, by the power of the holy ghost I destroy their evil powers right now in Jesus name. Amen.

SCRIPTURES FOR MEDITATION

Read and meditate on these scriptures below.

"He who is faithful in what is least is faithful also in much; and he who is unjust in what is least is unjust also in much." (Luke 16:10)

"He who has a slack hand becomes poor, But the hand of the diligent makes rich." (Proverbs 10:4)

"Blessings are on the head of the righteous, But violence covers the mouth of the wicked." (Proverbs 10:6)

"The memory of the righteous is blessed, But the name of the wicked will rot." (Proverbs 10:7)

CHAPTER 2

CONSISTENT PROMOTIONS & ADVERTISING

"Then the angel who talked with me answered and said to me, "Do you not know what these are?" And I said, "No, my Lord." So he answered and said to me: "This is the word of the Lord to Zerubbabel: 'Not by might nor by power, but by My Spirit,' Says the Lord of hosts. 'Who are you, O great mountain? Before Zerubbabel you shall become a plain! And he shall bring forth the capstone With shouts of "Grace, grace to it!" ' " Moreover the word of the Lord came to me, saying: "The hands of Zerubbabel Have laid the foundation of this temple; His hands shall also finish it. Then you will know That the Lord of hosts has sent Me to you. For who has despised the day of small things? For these seven rejoice to see The plumb line in the hand of Zerubbabel. They are the eyes of the Lord, Which scan to and fro throughout the whole earth."
(Zechariah 4:5-10)

Have you wondered why you changed your mind and bought a product you never wanted to buy and after using it, you discovered that it was actually a good product and you've been missing a lot for not having bought it since?

Have you sometimes turned off the TV or changed the channel just because you're tired of some ads that tend to annoy or irritate you? Or some ads you don't even know what they're talking about?

Have you bought a product just to give it a try only to discover that it was actually what you needed and what you've been looking for? And now you're so happy you came across that ad! How joyous it can be!

The truth is that we've all had this kind of experience. Sometimes you'll buy a product you never planned to buy just because it was promoted on TV or radio. At other times you'll buy a service you think it's the best just because of the way it was hyped in the media only to discover that the service delivery is completely dissatisfactory. What can you do?

As a business owner, you must realize that promotion is one of the greatest keys to success in your business. If people don't know your business, they won't patronize you. If they've never heard about you, how can they do business with you? If they can't trust you to deliver on your promises, how can they buy your products or services?

Promotion and advertising will do unimaginable wonders to your business. It can propel your business to a level you've never imagined. It will bring you clients you never thought could patronize you.

One thing promotion does is that it will create a massive awareness about your business and bring the kind of people who are willing and ready to pay for your products or services. A lot more people would be willing to do business with you if you promote and advertise your business, especially on different media platforms.

Ever wondered why the big telecom companies keep advertising their brand continuously even when they are yet to make any profit? Have you ever wondered why they take advertising so seriously that they have a separate team and budget for it?

The truth is that no matter how popular your business may be in your locality, there are people who would not have heard about you before. There is still room for improvement in acquiring more clients for your business. The more customers you have the more income you make and the more your business turnover.

It's not enough to promote and advertise your business, but to do it consistently. It's not enough to do it once and forget about it, but to continue to promote and advertise your business until you reach your goals.

You know one thing about how customers behave? It takes people a lot of time to finally decide to buy your products or services. This is especially if they've never patronized you before. People are usually skeptical of new things, new products or services. They are usually very conservative in spending their money, so to buy your products or services they would have to be convinced of its usefulness before they buy.

This is where promotions and advertising would come in. By promoting your business, you would make people develop a certain kind of likeness for your products which will make them decide to give it a try. If they try it once and you are able to make them trust your brand, it means you've made a customer for life.

He will continue to buy from you for as long as possible. And just as it's sometimes difficult to convince a new customer to buy from you it's also difficult to make a loyal and satisfied customer to leave a product or brand that is satisfying his needs to another brand he's not sure of.

He'd rather remain with the person or brand he knows than to gamble with someone he doesn't know! This is the mentality of many customers and that's why you see many companies having repeat customers continuously. It's because the companies have created a high level of trust in their customers and this loyalty and goodwill will keep bringing them sales for as long as possible.

Do not despise the days of little beginnings. Don't overlook promotions and advertising in your business. This is the key if you really want to succeed fast in your business.

It should not be a one-off thing. A one-off promotion campaign may not give you the desired results. It can sometimes be a waste of money. So to get the desired results, you must ensure that you do your business promotions and publicity for your business consistently until you see the desired results. It should be consistent and well planned, to be able to make the right impact.

You must realize that promotion is not only for big brands. Small businesses can also promote their products and services, even on the radio or TV or even on social media platforms via paid advertising. You can promote your business on social media platforms such as Nairaland, Instagram, Facebook, Twitter, whatsapp broadcast and email marketing campaigns.

This kind of advertising promotions is very effective in boosting your business and if you do this, a lot of people will get to know your business and would like to do business with you.

As you do this, commit everything you do to the Lord to guide you and bless the works of your hands. For the laborer is worthy of his wages, therefore you shall not labor in vain.

The Lord will bless your business and shower you with supernatural grace and favor in your business in Jesus name. Amen.

PRAYER TO ANNOUNCE YOU TO THE WORLD & FOR UPLIFTMENT IN YOUR BUSINESS

1. By the authority in the finished work of our Lord Jesus Christ on the Cross of Calvary, I decree and declare that your business will be announced to the world and people will know you and patronize you from far and wide in Jesus name. Amen.

2. I decree and declare the abundance of the grace of the Lord upon your life and upon your business and upon everything you lay your hands upon in Jesus name. Amen.

3. I decree and declare upliftment and financial rain in your business in Jesus name. Amen.

4. I decree and declare that the mercies of the Lord shall be with you in your business and in everything you do in Jesus name. Amen.

5. I command the eternal blessings of Abraham to follow you everywhere you go and I command the world to stand still for your sake everywhere you go in Jesus name. Amen.

SCRIPTURES FOR MEDITATION

Please read and meditate on the following scriptures.

"Unless the Lord builds the house, They labor in vain who build it; Unless the Lord guards the city, The watchman stays awake in vain." (Psalm 127:1)

"For the Scripture says, "You shall not muzzle an ox while it treads out the grain," and, "The laborer is worthy of his wages." " (1st Timothy 5:18)

CHAPTER 3

GOOD FINANCIAL INVESTMENT IN PROMOTIONS

"Good understanding gains favor, But the way of the unfaithful is hard." (Proverbs 13:15)

"Every prudent man acts with knowledge, But a fool lays open his folly." (Proverbs 13:16)

We earlier talked about the fact that you need to promote your business in the last chapter. Yes it's good to market and promote your business or products but is it any kind of promotion you should do?

Why is promotion so important that you need to invest a certain amount of money in promoting your business before you can get the desired results?

Why would a company spend a large chunk of its budget on promotions? Why are marketing and promotions so important in business that without them you may never make a single sale?

Why is that companies who massively promoted their products are making profits while those who never promoted theirs are making losses? Does it really matter if I promote my company with 2000 dollars or I promote it with 10,000 dollars? What difference does it make?

What if after spending 10,000 dollars in promoting my company and I decide that I'm not satisfied and then increase the ad budget to 50,000 dollars, will it make any difference in my business?

If we are selling similar products or services, can a company who spent 2000 dollars on their ads campaign be able to generate the kind of income my company would generate if I spent 50,000 dollars on promotion and advertising?

You might wonder why I titled this chapter "Good Financial Investment In Promotions"! The fact is that many business owners don't see promotions as an investment. They look at it as a waste or a gamble because they think they may never make the money back. But this is a very wrong mentality.

Just as you're investing money in stocks and shares, or you're investing money in several businesses, the same way you would have to invest a reasonable amount of money in promoting your business if you are really serious about making money from it.

If you view it as a waste or a gamble, it will be difficult to take the risk involved to spend a reasonable amount of money on promotions which holds the key to success in your business. No matter the kind of money you spend promoting your business, there's a high chance of making that money back 100 times over if your business is genuine and if all other factors are in place, especially proper packing of your business and good service delivery.

One good thing about promoting your business is that it has a multiplier effect on your business and would produce fruits with time. It's usually never a wasted effort when you properly market and promote your business. It's a good investment, especially if your aim is to grow big. Sometimes the results may not be immediate, but in the long run you will reap the fruits of your labor. So this is why I call it an investment.

My experience in business has shown that promotion is very important and necessary for every serious business person. I've learnt that promotion can be a shortcut to success in your business if properly done and if you have a reasonable budget for publicity. The budget has to be reasonable enough if you want to make an impact and get the kind of clients who would patronize you and take your business to the next level.

So you must see promotions as an investment if you must do it. Not every customer who contacts you when you promote your business will eventually patronize you. Some may not patronize you immediately, but might do so later when you don't even expect it.

But you must realize that some people may never get to know you unless you promote your business. The only thing that puts your business in the eyes of the public is through promotions and publicity.

So sometimes I laugh at people who place one slot advert in the newspapers or radio and expect to have many responses in their business. How can people respond when the advert is not adequate enough? If the ad investment is too small, then don't expect many responses.

If you placed only one or few slots, then you must know that only a limited number of people would see your ad. But if you have a good investment amount for your promotions, it will propel a wider circulation of your promotion campaign and more people will see it, especially those who need your products or services.

One of the most effective channels you can use for your business promotions is social media. Since millions of people are on social media platforms searching for what to buy, this is a great avenue to showcase your business.

A lot of people are making money advertising their business on whatsapp. On Instagram, there are lots of business opportunities and some people are making their income solely by being on Instagram.

Aside from what you can do with your business by being active on social media, you should make use of paid advertising to grow your business. You can't do it alone, you need a team to work with you to help you grow your business and take your brand to greater heights.

You can start from a smaller ad budget and then gradually increase it as you go. But for you to make a certain kind of money in your business, you must invest a reasonable budget in not just your entire business but also in promotions and advertising.

The Lord will give you the wisdom and grace to do the right thing in your business that will move you forward in Jesus name. Amen.

God bless you.

PRAYER FOR FINANCIAL FAVOR TO EXPAND YOUR BUSINESS

1. I decree and declare that the Lord will open the heavens and send you help from His Sanctuary. I decree that the Lord will send you a helper that will change your life and financial situation in Jesus name. Amen.

2. I decree and declare that your business will boom and expand beyond your own imagination to every part of the country and to the entire world in Jesus name. Amen.

3. I decree and declare that the Lord will bless you with the financial resources to expand your business in Jesus name. Amen.

4. I decree and declare that any power of limitation and setback in your business be destroyed right now in Jesus name. Amen.

5. Every plot of the enemy to make you remain in one point for life without progress, I destroy their evil plans against your life and I set you free right now in Jesus name. Amen.

SCRIPTURES FOR MEDITATION

Please read and meditate on the following scriptures.

"The plans of the diligent lead surely to plenty, But those of everyone who is hasty, surely to poverty. (Proverbs 21:5)

"The wise store up choice food and olive oil, but fools gulp theirs down." (Proverbs 21:20)

"Invest in seven ventures, yes, in eight; you do not know what disaster may come upon the land." (Ecclesiastes 11:2)

"A faithful man will abound with blessings, but he who makes haste to be rich will not go unpunished. (Proverbs 28:20)

CHAPTER 4

LONG PERIOD OF PROMOTIONS

"But let patience have its perfect work, that you may be perfect and complete, lacking nothing." (James 1:4)

What do you think will happen to your business if you run a massive Facebook ad for one year? If I do a marketing and promotions campaign for my business for one year on different digital platforms and you do the same thing for your business for three months, do you think both of us will have the same responses from customers?

When it comes to conversion to actual sales from such campaigns, do you think we'll be on the same level? Do you think a three months marketing promotion can be compared to a one year promotion? Does time duration really matter here?

Does it matter how long you create awareness about your business? Can you leverage on your past reputation and decide not to bother about how you market and promote your business going forward?

Yes we know that promotion is the key to success in your business, but does it really matter how you go about it? Does it matter how long you do it and can it have an impact on your business, especially if not done adequately?

The truth is that when you want to promote your business, you must have a high projection for the future. Your aim should be the long term benefits of your promotion campaign. This is because sometimes you may not get the returns on investment immediately. If you set out with the expectation of an immediate gain, you may be seriously disappointed. Yes this can be very frustrating when the returns are not coming in as you expect.

Many businesses have been frustrated due to this kind of wrong mentality by the owners. They think that by placing ads in the newspapers or radio or on online platforms for a short while will bring in a lot of responses or sales that will turn their business around. But guess what? Many have been really disappointed when they couldn't even make a single sale after spending some money on these kinds of short promotion advertising.

No one wishes to have this kind of ugly experience in business, but it happens often, especially to small businesses and people who have little or no experience in marketing. They just want to gamble with the little money at their disposal and see if it works! No, it may never work the way you expect.

So it's not enough to promote your business, it's often better to do it for a reasonably long period of time in order to harness the immense benefits of repetitiveness of such ad campaigns. The more you repeat it on the same platform, the more people will begin to take it seriously.

The more they see it, the more likely they are to take action and contact you or buy your product or service. How can you make a sale with a one-off advert? How can people take you seriously when they only saw your advert once and may have even forgotten the content of your promotion?

It will take some people who are slow in decision making to see your advert for up to 7 times consecutively before they can be convinced to contact you or even think of buying. It will take some people to see several ad campaigns of a product or service before they could even consider giving it a try.

If you can afford to run your ad campaign for one year, then why are you running it for one month? If you can afford to run it on multiple platforms, then why are you running it only on one platform? Do you know that if you run a good promotion campaign for your business for one year, you can be making sales from such campaign for the next five years or more?

There's always a multiplier effect advertising has on a business such that it can continue to bring clients for you for many years to come, even when you've forgotten about the advert you did many years ago. It's so powerful to promote your business, especially if you do it properly and use a good and credible platform.

Long periods of promotions will expose your business to so many people. It will bring your business in contact with both the serious and unserious ones who will respond to your advert campaigns. It's left for you to weed them out because it's not possible for all of them to eventually patronize you, no matter how hard you try to convince them.

I would say that promotion constitutes at least 70% of the work needed to be done in your business to make it have consistent sales and a good turnover. Every serious business needs to be well promoted, especially in this era of social media where almost everybody is online looking for one opportunity or the other.

Sometimes social media promotion is even faster in converting your prospects to sales. And the beauty of it is that you can decide to start small and gradually scale it up, especially if you're on a limited budget. But your best bet is to have a reasonable budget for your business promotions and then do it for as long as possible until you begin to see tangible results.

And even when you begin to see tangible results, don't relax, continue to promote your business for a long period of time or indefinitely if you can. If you do this, a time will come when you will begin to earn a consistent income on your efforts. This consistent income can be monthly, quarterly or yearly, depending on the kind of business you do.

The word of the Lord says we should persevere and that those who persevere and don't give up too soon will have a good reward. There's always light at the end of the tunnel for those who keep the hope alive and don't give up, no matter the circumstances.

There's always a good reward for you if you put in the effort needed to achieve your goals and then don't give up when you get to a point where you expect to achieve the aim but it's not yet forthcoming. It will come, just hold on and trust the Lord that He is with you all the way, no matter the situation.

The Lord be with you in your business and send His angels to bring you favor from heaven.

The Lord will shower you with mercy and bring you the kind of clients you need in your business. I decree that genuine clients will seek you to do business with you and favor you in Jesus name. Amen.

The peace of the Lord be with you in Jesus name. Amen.

PRAYER FOR HEALING AND DELIVERANCE OVER YOUR LIFE AND FAMILY

1. By the authority in the Blood of Jesus Christ shed on the cross of Calvary, be healed and delivered right now in Jesus name. Amen.

2. I decree supernatural healing and deliverance into your life and your family right now in Jesus name. Amen.

3. Any plot of the enemy to cause hidden ailments in your life and your family in order to make you keep spending all your money in hospitals, I cancel such evil plan against your life right now and I set you and your family free by the authority in the Blood of Jesus Christ shed on the cross of Calvary. Amen.

4. Any plot of the enemy to cause you or any member of your family accident or sudden death, I destroy their evil plans right now in Jesus name. Amen.

5. Any plot of the enemy to cause trouble, rancor, disaffection or hatred between you and your family and your staff in your business, I destroy all their evil plans right now in Jesus name. Amen.

6. Since whatever affects your health or your family can eventually affect your business or source of income, therefore I decree and declare a sound mind and sound health into your life and family right now in Jesus name. Amen.

SCRIPTURES FOR MEDITATION
Please read and meditate on the following scriptures.

"And He said to them, "Which of you shall have a friend, and go to him at midnight and say to him, 'Friend, lend me three loaves; for a friend of mine has come to me on his journey, and I have nothing to set before him'; and he will answer from within and say, 'Do not trouble me; the door is now shut, and my children are with me in bed; I cannot rise and give to you'? I say to you, though he will not rise and give to him because he is his friend, yet because of his persistence he will rise and give him as many as he needs. "So I say to you, ask, and it will be given to you; seek, and you will find; knock, and it will be opened to you. For everyone who asks receives, and he who seeks finds, and to him who knocks it will be opened. (Luke 11:5-10)

"And let us not grow weary while doing good, for in due season we shall reap if we do not lose heart." (Galatians 6:9)

"Then He spoke a parable to them, that men always ought to pray and not lose heart,
saying: "There was in a certain city a judge who did not fear God nor regard man. Now there was a widow in that city; and she came to him, saying, 'Get justice for me from my adversary.' And he would not for a while; but afterward he said within himself, 'Though I do not fear God nor regard man, yet because this widow troubles me I will avenge her, lest by her continual coming she weary me.' " Then the Lord said, "Hear what the unjust judge said. And shall God not avenge His own elect who cry out day and night to Him, though He bears long with them? I tell you that He will avenge them speedily. Nevertheless, when the Son of Man comes, will He really find faith on the earth?" (Luke 18:1-8)

"Therefore, my beloved brethren, be steadfast, immovable, always abounding in the work of the Lord, knowing that your labor is not in vain in the Lord." (1st Corinthians 15:58)

CHAPTER 5

HAVING MULTIPLE PRODUCTS OR SERVICES

"In the morning sow your seed, And in the evening do not withhold your hand; For you do not know which will prosper, Either this or that, Or whether both alike will be good." (Ecclesiates 11:6)

Have you noticed that companies that have several multiple products make the most sales? Do you know that if you offer several services in your business, the tendency is that when a client comes to your office and decides he doesn't like your offer on the service he came to inquire about, he might just pay for another service if you offer several services?

Now I keep wondering why some business owners will just decide to offer just one product or service when they could make more money by offering several of them at a reasonably cheaper cost since they will use the same facilities they already have to offer more to their customers.

One of the surest ways to make consistent income in your business is to offer multiple products and services to your customers. Let them have several options and varieties.

In fact by having several options for them, it will boost your customers' regard for your business and also boost your credibility as a serious business entity. Some people will even patronize you based on the fact that they came to your shop and saw several varieties of options available for them to choose from. If they come and see your shop scanty, it can portray you as an unserious business person. It can make you lose some customers.

That's why you see a lot of shops filled to the brim with goods, sometimes these goods are just decorations, the main products may be in the warehouse, but they must ensure that their shops are stocked with at least the basic goods that customers always request for, so that they won't lose any sale.

If you produce items for sale, it's also very good to have multiple products and expand your customer base because there will be more people who may not need what you produce but variety will give them different choices. But most times it's better to do this in related fields.

Likewise, if you offer services, offering multiple services will make people have a one-stop shop where they can order a lot of your services which they would have bought elsewhere if you hadn't diversified your portfolio. It's best to offer your services in related fields because it can be confusing for your customers when your services are in different fields. It could make you look like a jack of all trades and this can damage your credibility.

Now we've seen companies who offer products and services at the same time. They not only have multiple lines of products but they also offer several services which gives their customers lots of options to choose from. This may not be an easy thing to achieve, but the reward for such efforts will pay off in the long run.

One of the reasons to have multiple products and services on offer is that business can sometimes be very unpredictable and the product you think will sell well may not even sell while the one you never ever imagined would sell could be the one people would like so much and would end up selling so much more than others.

You really can't tell what people would like since customers have several preferences. Just as people are diverse in their thinking, the same way they are different in their choices. What one person doesn't like is exactly what another is looking for, so sometimes it's difficult to understand people.

So your best bet is to make sure you offer several options to your customers and let them have a reason to come back again to patronize you. Most times they may not even be aware that you offer other products or services until you introduce it to them and convince them to buy from you. People will always buy from those they know or those who have satisfied their needs before.

So diversification is very important to success in your business. Starting small is good, but when you eventually start, are you willing to scale up your business and diversify into other areas where you can make even more money than where you started? This is because as you go, opportunities will come in other areas and if you consider them and invest your resources in trying them out, this can be the turning point for your business.

Don't be afraid to try new things in your business. Many people who have tried new things have ended up taking their business to unimaginable levels.

The fear of failure is one of the reasons why many people don't want to diversify their portfolio offers with respect to their products or services. But it's better to try and fail and learn from it than never to try at all.

You will still be better off than the person who never tried at all because you would have acquired some life experiences he doesn't have. This experience can still help you succeed sooner or later in the course of your business.

The reason why some people have not been able to make headway in their business is because they are simply not willing to diversify and try new things. But as they say, change is constant and things will never remain the same. The earlier you're willing to embrace relevant change in your business the better. Take note that such change must be relevant, reasonable and ethical before you can embrace it. It must be able to add value to your business.

But many people reject change. They are not willing to even improve on the things they are doing and this is a recipe for disaster since the world is constantly evolving.

As the world keeps changing everyday, then be ready to change alongside and try new things that will appeal to your customers more. This is a sure way to retain your old customers and acquire new ones. But remember that whatever changes you embrace in your business must conform to the word of God.

You can't just embrace any change because the world is doing it. It must conform to the will of God and must not be the will of man. It must be in line with what God wants for your life, so that He can bless the works of your hands.

You will succeed in Jesus name. Amen.

PRAYER OF IMPARTATION TO RECEIVE UNIQUE BUSINESS IDEAS

1. I decree and declare that from now on you will receive dreams and visions and divine ideas on how to move your business and life forward in Jesus name. Amen.

2. I decree and declare that the Lord will give you great and unique ideas on how to produce multiple products and services that will announce your business and bring you great fortune in Jesus name. Amen.

3. I decree and declare that the Lord will bless you with immense business wisdom and people from far and wide will seek you to consult your wisdom in setting up their own businesses in Jesus name. Amen.

4. I decree that from today, your business ideas will take you far and wide and make you meet with important personalities in your country and around the world in Jesus name. Amen.

5. I decree that the Lord will send you people who are financially capable to help you implement your business ideas and to expand your business in Jesus name. Amen.

SCRIPTURES FOR MEDITATION

Please meditate on the scriptures below and pray with them.

"And you shall remember the Lord your God, for it is He who gives you power to get wealth, that He may establish His covenant which He swore to your fathers, as it is this day." (Deuteronomy 8:18)

"Better is a little with righteousness, Than vast revenues without justice." (Proverbs 16:8)

"In the morning sow your seed, And in the evening do not withhold your hand; For you do not know which will prosper, Either this or that, Or whether both alike will be good." (Ecclesiates 11:6)

"And whatever you do in word or deed, do all in the name of the Lord Jesus, giving thanks to God the Father through Him." (Collosians 3:17)

"Without counsel, plans go awry, But in the multitude of counselors they are established." (Proverbs 15:22)

"For as the body without the spirit is dead, so faith without works is dead also." (James 2:26)

CHAPTER 6

PROPER BUSINESS BRANDING

"Whatever your hand finds to do, do it with your might; for there is no work or device or knowledge or wisdom in the grave where you are going." (Ecclesiates 9:10)

Do you know that some big businesses that have become national brands today started from just one room? And guess what? Some of the people who own these brands didn't even know it would one day become big!

They just started by giving it a try and with time, it grew to become popular and expanded to other cities and towns.

Can you imagine a single person starting a small business in a room and then after a while, this same business now becomes big that it now employs hundreds and thousands of people across the nation?

Some people mistakenly think that this kind of achievement is only meant for some kind of people or for some special kind of individuals but that's not true. Your own business can achieve it too if you do the right things and if you're diligent enough.

You can't go big if you haven't started small. It's advisable to learn the ropes first, so that by the time you get big in your business, you would have learnt a lot of things you need to know about the nature of the business.

To do certain kinds of businesses successfully requires some kind of experience as well as trial and errors here and there, but in all, you must learn something to do something.

A lot of people fail in business because they are not willing to learn the ropes from those who took their time to learn and practise it.

Many even failed to read relevant books that would teach them about the business and they just assume they can do it. But after some years of venturing into it, they would fail woefully. Pathetic! This will never be your portion in Jesus name. Amen.

Now one of the most important things you must do in your business if you're really serious about taking it to the next level is to properly brand your business to have a credible, reliable and positive image in the eyes of the people.

The reputation of business is very important, just as your own reputation is important because it will rub off on your business. In fact your own personal reputation is even the first thing people will check to ensure your company is run by credible people.

If people discover your business or company is filled with shady people, they will not like to do business with you.

To succeed in your business, you must painstakingly make efforts to build a reputable brand that will stand the test of time.

You must know how to develop your business to a level where a lot of people will be willing to do business with you because your business has credibility. You must garner enough goodwill from people and this can be done through quality service delivery and building trust in your customers.

Tips For Proper Business Branding

1. Beautiful office. Your office must be beautiful and attractive with modern facilities. Not having an office where people can contact you is a turn off for most clients.

Many small businesses struggle to have a presentable office and some don't even have yet.

This is a very important aspect of your business, without which some people will never do business with you, no matter how good your services are.

2. Beautifully designed, attractive and easy to navigate website. Put all your products and services on your website for the world to see.

If you want to reach the world, you must have a business website where you'll showcase all your business activities, your products, services and offerings.

3. Beautiful color combination for your brand. Ensure you use attractive colors to design your brand materials and be consistent with the colors you use for your brand.

4. Well designed company or business logo. This is equally very important because the first thing people will see about your business is your company logo. It must be professionally designed to project the right image about your business and what you do.

5. Company professional letterhead. Send all letters and correspondence via your company letter headed paper.

6. Ensure your phone lines are always reachable at all times during working hours.

7. Ensure you have a beautifully designed business card, Invoice Book, Handbills, Banners, etc.

8. Ensure prompt delivery of ordered products and services. Delay in delivery is a turn off for most clients. They will not come back if they had a bad experience with you.

9. Create a positive image for your business or brand via quality service delivery and quality products.

You must market and sell your business with every opportunity that comes your way. Spread the word about your business. The more people know your business, the more likely your brand will register in the minds of the people.

10. You must have a corporate bank account. Don't use your personal bank account to receive funds for your business.

You must ensure you have your business or company bank account because it's more professional to use your company account to receive business funds than using your personal account.

Many people will not even agree to pay into your personal account for a business transaction. It makes you look corporate and gives you more credibility to have a company account where all payments are made to you.

11. Proper training and retraining of your staff on work ethics and customer relations. This is also very important for your business. The absence of good staff alone can crumble any business no matter how you market and promote the business or company.

May the Lord will give you the wisdom to navigate through the business environment and the grace to attract the right kind of people that will help you take your business to greater heights in Jesus name. Amen

PRAYER FOR SUPERNATURAL GRACE TO SERVE GOD IN YOUR BUSINESS

1. I pray for you today, that as you do your business, may the Lord will give you the grace not to be misled by things of this world in Jesus name. Amen.

2. May the Lord grant you the eternal wisdom to discern the truth and to discern the kinds of people you meet everyday in your business in Jesus name. Amen.

3. May the Lord grant you the wisdom to know the proper way to brand your business, to conform with the word of the Lord and not to please the world in Jesus name. Amen.

4. May the Lord grant you the eternal wisdom not to be deceived by the lust of the flesh, the lust for money and the lust for material things which are plots of the enemy to trap your soul and make you miss God.

5. May the Lord grant you the wisdom to brand your business in the right way that would attract the right kind of customers that the Lord has destined to meet with you in Jesus name. Amen.

SCRIPTURES FOR MEDITATION
Please meditate on these scriptures and pray with them.

"Commit your works to the Lord, And your thoughts will be established." (Proverbs 16:3)

"He who is faithful in what is least is faithful also in much; and he who is unjust in what is least is unjust also in much." (Luke 16:10)

"And do not be conformed to this world, but be transformed by the renewing of your mind, that you may prove what is that good and acceptable and perfect will of God." (Romans 12:2)

"For I know the thoughts that I think toward you, says the Lord, thoughts of peace and not of evil, to give you a future and a hope." (Jeremiah 29:11)

"But whoever keeps His word, truly the love of God is perfected in him. By this we know that we are in Him. He who says he abides in Him ought himself also to walk just as He walked." (1st John 2:5-6)

"The Lord is my shepherd; I shall not want. He makes me to lie down in green pastures; He leads me beside the still waters." (Psalm 23:1-2)

"Be exalted, O God, above the heavens; Let Your glory be above all the earth." (Psalm 57:5)

CHAPTER 7

GOOD CUSTOMER SERVICE

"Learn to do good; Seek justice, Rebuke the oppressor; Defend the fatherless, Plead for the widow. "Come now, and let us reason together," Says the Lord, "Though your sins are like scarlet, They shall be as white as snow; Though they are red like crimson, They shall be as wool. If you are willing and obedient, You shall eat the good of the land;" (Isaiah 1:17-19)

Have you ever contacted a person for business and the way they responded to you made you so disappointed in them? Have you had this kind of experience before? How did you feel? Did you feel like spending your hard earned money to buy their products or services after such awful customer service?

I wonder what makes some people think that they're so indispensable that they would begin to treat others so shabbily when inquiries are made about the business or product they advertised.

After spending a lot of money to advertise your business, people now contact you and all you can do is to talk to them very rudely just because they are not willing to pay your exorbitant price or because they are asking relevant questions about your business. Is this not a red signal to them that there's every tendency that you won't even deliver on your promises?

This is a sign that you're not a reliable business and a lot of people will never call you again after that negative first impression. You must watch your every move and how you answer or interact with your customers.

The first impression you give a customer matters a lot and it can sometimes determine if they would stay with you or look elsewhere to get what they want.

Remember that customers can sometimes be unpredictable in their decisions, so you'll compound it when you treat them shabbily. They will never come back to you anymore.

They would rather buy from someone whose products or services are not even as quality as yours and who treats them like a king than to buy from you whose products are the best but you treat them like trash. No customer will take this, no matter how they need the product or service.

If they need it so much, they would rather look for an alternative, even if it might cost them more, they won't mind the extra money they would spend to buy it where they are respected and appreciated. This is a key element of selling that many people in business do not know.

It's not enough to be an entrepreneur. It's not enough to have a business. It matters a lot to mind the way you treat and attend to your customers and prospects. Put yourself in their shoes and see if you would like to be treated that way! A king should be treated like a king and not as a slave. Is it not an abomination to treat a king like a slave?

They are actually the king in your business. Without them you will go out of business. You are there in business to serve their needs and the moment they notice that you're taking them for granted, even the ones who are loyal customers will switch their loyalty and find a better alternative.

If you treat your customers like trash just like some ignorant people who own businesses do and who think they are indispensable, you would soon find out that you are dispensable. They can even go to a far place to find an alternative that will suit their needs, even if it costs them more.

WHY MANY BUSINESSES CRASH

One of the reasons why some small businesses can never become big is because they are too proud of their little achievements and they now start treating customers like trash.

When they initially started they were begging to have customers, but eventually when they started making it, they now changed and became hostile to the customers! Can you imagine? Is this not preposterous to say the least?

The mentality of many business owners is not to grow big. Their mentality is very limited by their narrow thinking. They think they can't become big or expand to other parts of the country. So they limit themselves by their thinking. And when they start making little money, they will feel on top of the world and would begin to treat others, especially their customers with contempt.

This is the reason many people remain in their poor and meager state with their businesses and after sometime, instead of the business to be growing bigger, it would rather crash and they would go back to square one and eventually fold up the business.

Some people who own businesses fail to realize that the fact that a business is making money today does not mean it cannot crash tomorrow or in the nearest future.

If you fail to put the right things in place in your business, it can still crash and fold up even if you're making a lot of money from it right now. It doesn't matter how much you're making currently. Have we not seen big business organizations fold up before our own very eyes?

It doesn't matter how big you are as a business, the moment your customers no longer matter to you because you've already made a lot of money, just forget it, you will crash sooner or later, except you quickly realize your mistakes and retrace your steps and begin to treat your customers very well.

Why should you even treat a king like a slave? Have you ever seen where a king is treated like a slave? Can anyone try this anywhere without dire consequences?

When people say that the customer is a king, this is a great parable that many small businesses fail to understand. They will start their business and crash within a short time.

They would invest a lot of money in business and all the money would go down the drain because of their arrogance to their customers and their inability to humble themselves in business.

Pride goes before a fall and many people are going for deliverance prayers to know what was responsible for their business crashing but they failed to realize that they are the architect of their own misfortune.

They are looking for a prophet to tell them why it happened but many of them will fall into the hands of false prophets who would lie to them that someone in their village is responsible for their downfall, just to hoodwink them of the little money remaining with them, whereas they failed to realize that they caused their problems by themselves due to their ignorance, arrogance, pride and negligence.

Many people are in this situation today whose businesses have crashed in many parts of the country and they would not know that it may just be a thing as negligible as pride that caused their problems.

It may just be a customer they insulted or looked down upon, just because perhaps he could not afford to pay for their item, and their problem started from there, and since then all they had would just go down the drain and they would never be able to gather anything in their entire life until they first realize what the cause of the problem is, then repent of that pride and then plead for forgiveness genuinely with a brokenness to God for allowing the devil to use them.

It can even be worse for some people if the customer they insulted is a man of God but unknown to them. Some could suffer this calamity for the rest of their lives, but they would not even know what caused the problem in the first place. And if a person does not even know what caused his problems, how can he be able to find the solution?

This is a mystery that many business owners don't know and they keep wasting time and money acquiring businesses and building business empires that would eventually crash due to a supposedly small or negligent mistake they've made in the past which will crop up one day and crumble the business despite all the efforts they've made to sustain the business.

PRAYERS TO CANCEL PAST MISTAKES THAT WANT TO CRASH YOUR BUSINESS

1. Every mistake that you've made in the past that is gearing up to crumble your life and business, I cancel it by the authority in the Blood of Jesus Christ. Amen.

2. Every little thing or error that looks so negligible to you but looks so great in the eyes of God which Satan with his demons are planning to use it against your destiny, right now by the authority in the Blood of Jesus Christ shed on the cross of Calvary, I cancel it and set you free right now in Jesus name. Amen.

3. Every person you have insulted knowingly or unknowingly in the course of your life or business which the devil is using against you, right now I cancel it and set you free in Jesus name. Amen.

4. Every plot of the enemy with his demons to scatter your business, to crash your business and make you go back to square one, I take authority over such plots against your life and business right now and scatter such plans right now and I set you free in Jesus name. Amen.

5. Every satanic and demonic curse upon your life and business, by the authority in the Blood of Jesus Christ shed on the cross of Calvary, I cancel it right now in Jesus name. Amen.

6. Any powers that have vowed to torment your life and business, I destroy it with holy ghost fire right now in Jesus name. Amen.

7. Any demonic or Satanic powers that have held your life hostage, I command it to die by fire right now in Jesus name. Amen.

8. By the authority in the Blood of Jesus Christ shed on the cross of Calvary, I set you free from all evil spells, curses and plots against your life and against your business, from any demonic coven, from any monitoring spirit, from all demonic altars, from any witchcraft coven, from any occultic coven, from the marine kingdom, from the powers of the air, from the powers of the forests, from the powers of the land, from ancestral curses, from any human being living or dead, from any soul tie or demonic covenant you entered into knowingly or unknowingly, I set you free right now in the mighty name of Jesus Christ. Amen.

SCRIPTURES FOR REGULAR READING FOR BUSINESS SUCCESS
As the Lord directs as I write this, please read these scriptures below regularly on a daily basis for your business success and financial breakthrough.

Read them every night before you sleep and every morning when you wake up and pray with them.

Psalm 23.
Psalm 24.
Psalm 91.
Psalm 32:7
Psalm 121.
Psalm 1.
Psalm 145.

Do it for 30 days consecutively and see what happens. As you do it, do it with faith and the Lord will take care of your situation in Jesus name. Amen.

The peace of the Lord be with you in Jesus name. Amen.

SCRIPTURES FOR MEDITATION

Please read and meditate on these scriptures and pray with them from time to time.

"And just as you want men to do to you, you also do to them likewise." (Luke 6:31)

"As each one has received a gift, minister it to one another, as good stewards of the manifold grace of God." (1st Peter 4:10)

"Fight the good fight of faith, lay hold on eternal life, to which you were also called and have confessed the good confession in the presence of many witnesses." (1st Timothy 6:12)

"For God so loved the world that He gave His only begotten Son, that whoever believes in Him should not perish but have everlasting life. For God did not send His Son into the world to condemn the world, but that the world through Him might be saved. He who believes in Him is not condemned; but he who does not believe is condemned already, because he has not believed in the name of the only begotten Son of God." (John 3:16-18)

"For by grace you have been saved through faith, and that not of yourselves; it is the gift of God, not of works, lest anyone should boast. For we are His workmanship, created in Christ Jesus for good works, which God prepared beforehand that we should walk in them." (Ephesians 2:8-10)

CHAPTER 8

GOOD PRICING SYSTEM

"Dishonest scales are an abomination to the Lord, But a just weight is His delight." (Proverbs 11:1)

"'You shall do no injustice in judgment, in measurement of length, weight, or volume. You shall have honest scales, honest weights, an honest ephah, and an honest hin: I am the Lord your God, who brought you out of the land of Egypt.'" (Leviticus 19:35-36)

"For the love of money is a root of all kinds of evil, for which some have strayed from the faith in their greediness, and pierced themselves through with many sorrows." (1st Timothy 6:10)

Have you noticed that the prices of goods and services are always on the increase? Have you ever seen a situation where prices keep falling even when people's incomes are increasing? The norm is that prices usually increase with time, irrespective of whether people's incomes increase or not, irrespective of whether people get jobs or not.

I often wonder why prices keep going up, and now the cost of many items are basically out of the reach of many people. So a lot of businesses are struggling to survive due to the effect of the Coronavirus pandemic which took the world by storm.

But despite many businesses closing shop, a lot of other establishments are springing up and growing to become large organizations. So despite many have been adversely affected, a lot are having a field day and making so much returns. It's a case of one man's meat being another man's poison.

If both of us are manufacturers and I decide to sell my product at $50 and you decide to sell yours at $70 despite both products have the same quality, what is the tendency that a customer who is aware of the two different prices would buy from you, knowing fully well that he will derive the same quality and benefit from each item irrespective of where he decides to buy it?

If he eventually decides to buy it from you despite knowing he could get it cheaper elsewhere, then there must have been some perceived value he attached to your product that made him buy it despite the higher cost. Or perhaps he is unaware that both are of the same quality and would give the same benefit to him.

One of the most important decisions you can make as an entrepreneur is to decide the right prices to sell your products and services. This can be the determining factor and can make or mar your business. In fact price is so important that any little increase or reduction in your price can increase or decrease your returns.

Your customers will always compare prices and decide which to go for. They know the prices of your competitors and other businesses in your line of trade, but they will only decide to buy from you if your price is right for them or if your item provides more value to them than others.

They don't ever want to lose their money no matter how small, so your price can make the difference in your quest for business success. If you get your price right, you've already won a lot of customers without knowing because sooner or later they would come and buy from you, if not for anything, but because of your lower prices despite providing the same quality with those who charge higher prices.

The best thing you can do to your business is to ensure your prices are moderate, while providing excellent quality products and services. If people know they can always buy at lower prices from you, they will flock your shop and you will sell out your goods faster than others, thereby leading to high turnover for your business. This is very important for business growth.

Instead of selling one item per day in your shop at an exorbitant price, why not sell ten of such items at cheaper prices per day and make more money? Instead of selling twenty items per month at an exorbitant price, why not sell a hundred per month at a cheaper price? The more you sell, the more turnover for your business.

If you're a starter, it's almost mandatory to start with low prices if you want to sustain your business and if you want people to know you. They won't know you unless something draws them to you and the easiest way is to attract them through your lower prices.

Have you not seen some businesses who sell at exorbitant prices but they still lack and are unable to make headway whereas some who sell at lower prices are making headway more than them?

They think that by being greedy and by increasing their prices so high would make the difference but they failed to realize that sometimes blessing in business is not dependent on how high your price is.

Sometimes blessing in business is dependent on how contented you are with the little God has given you and your desire to acquire wealth through honesty and genuine means instead of through cheating and trying to cut corners at the expense of others.

When you cheat others to acquire wealth it will not last. It's dangerous for your life. It's a snare for your soul by the enemy to trap your life into the bondage of the god of mammon. Beware!

You will make money in your business if you're faithful and diligent enough. Whatever will be for you will not pass you by, you will get it. But whatever is not meant for you, remove your eyes from it, don't take it because it's a trap of the enemy against your life and against your destiny.

The peace of the Lord be with you in Jesus name. Amen.

DELIVERANCE PRAYERS AGAINST GREED AND COVETOUSNESS

1. Every evil arrow from the enemy that has been programmed into your life to make you take what does not belong to you, I destroy it in Jesus name. Amen.

2. Every evil covenant you have entered into knowingly or unknowingly by taking items or properties that do not belong to you, I cancel it with the Blood of Jesus Christ. Amen.

3. Every evil altar dedicated to monitor your life and business to make you make a mistake that could cost you your life, I smash such evil after into pieces right now in Jesus name. Amen.

4. Any demon or evil spirit that has been assigned to monitor your life and to influence you negatively to take what does not belong to you, I command it to die by fire in Jesus name. Amen.

5. Since covetousness is equal to the sin of idolatry, therefore anything that will make you to covet what God has not put into your hands thereby committing the sin of idolatry, I cancel it right now in Jesus name. Amen.

6. Every evil plot of the enemy and his demons to cause the sin of greed in your life and make you lust after material things to ensnare your soul, I cancel it right now in Jesus name. Amen.

7. By the authority in the Blood of Jesus Christ shed on the cross of Calvary, I set you free from all evil chains of the enemy holding your life and business captive in Jesus name. Amen.

SCRIPTURES FOR MEDITATION
Please read and meditate on the following scriptures and pray with them.

"Be anxious for nothing, but in everything by prayer and supplication, with thanksgiving, let your requests be made known to God; and the peace of God, which surpasses all understanding, will guard your hearts and minds through Christ Jesus." (Phillipians 4:6-7)

"Better is the poor who walks in his integrity Than one perverse in his ways, though he be rich." (Proverbs 28:6)

"One who increases his possessions by usury and extortion Gathers it for him who will pity the poor." (Proverbs 28:8)

"'You shall not steal, nor deal falsely, nor lie to one another.'" (Leviticus 19:11)

"Do not lie to one another, since you have put off the old man with his deeds, and have put on the new man who is renewed in knowledge according to the image of Him who created him," (Colossians 3:9-10)

"Indeed the wages of the laborers who mowed your fields, which you kept back by fraud, cry out; and the cries of the reapers have reached the ears of the Lord of Sabaoth." (James 5:4)

"Do not overwork to be rich; Because of your own understanding, cease!" *(Proverbs 23:4)*

CHAPTER 9

STUDYING YOUR CUSTOMERS

"Who may ascend into the hill of the Lord? Or who may stand in His holy place? He who has clean hands and a pure heart, Who has not lifted up his soul to an idol, Nor sworn deceitfully. He shall receive blessing from the Lord, And righteousness from the God of his salvation." (Psalm 24:3-5)

One of the most complex creatures on the surface of this earth is human beings. Humans are so complex in nature that it's really difficult to understand them. No matter how hard you try, you can't understand everybody.

People change often and if you think you understand a person, you may just be surprised that after a long while the person might have changed a lot in their personality. As the days go by, people evolve and discard their old self and put on new personalities. This is one of the things that make people complex in nature and difficult to understand.

One of the important elements of business is to know your customer. Every business entrepreneur deals with different kinds of people everyday. No matter your experience in business, as long as you're still interacting with people, you will continue to meet people with all kinds of strange behavioral tendencies which you've never come across before.

If you think you've seen it all, just hold it because sooner or later you're likely to meet someone you've never met before from whom you will learn something new.

To be able to sell your products and services well, you need to know a lot about your customers. You must make a conscious effort to study them if you must remain in business.

What kind of people are you dealing with and why are they even patronizing you? Why would they come all the way and bypass all the shops selling similar products and then come only to your shop to buy from you?

It means there must be something special you're offering them that others don't offer. It means that there is a special thing that magnets them to your business to patronize you at the expense of other competitors.

If you want to go far in your business as an entrepreneur, don't be carried away by the sales you're making. Don't let it make you relax and not plan ahead to find out certain things about your business that can improve it.

You must constantly do your customer survey and gather all the necessary information about your business and about your customers and use it to plan ahead, so that you can be ahead of your competitors.

Since human beings are complex by nature, you must devise a strategic plan to get them to reveal to you certain things you would not have ordinarily known.

You can achieve this through having good relationships with your customers and through this, they will be free to tell you their mind. Be friendly with them and be willing to bear rejection from lots of them. Not all will reciprocate your gesture for sure, but don't worry, carry on to the next person.

Succeeding in business is a combination of several factors which help a business to succeed. But the most important element of any business is the customers and satisfying their needs.

If you don't have the zeal to run your business, and you're too skeptical and negative minded from the onset, it will be difficult for you to make a headway. This is because you need a strong determination to do it and a positive mindset to achieve your goals irrespective of the odds.

Above all, you need the supernatural hand of the Lord to be with you in your business and no power of darkness can come near you. It is well with you in Jesus name.

The peace of the Lord be with you in Jesus name. Amen.

Tips On Business & Customer Survey

1. Study your customers to know their feedback towards your business or company.

2. Study your customers regularly to know what they want and find a way to give them what they want.

3. Study your customers to know their attitude and views towards your newly introduced product or service.

4. Find out from your customers what they think about your competitors. This relevant information will help you to know how to adjust your own business.

5. Create products and services that meet the yearnings and aspirations of your customers.

6. Create products and services, where possible, that your customers can afford.

7. Create products and services suitable for a certain category or group of customers.

8. Create products and services which are not common, that are rare to come by, so that you will be unique and indispensable in that line of business.

9. Ask your customers relevant probing questions and follow-up questions to gather information about your business, the industry you operate in and about the economy in general. Use questionnaires when necessary to have a documented entry of their responses.

10. Find out from them what kind of product or service they would like to be introduced by your company into the market. Most times it's based on people's needs that products and services are created. You can be the first to create a product or service that people need in your country. Yes you can!

PRAYERS FOR SUPERNATURAL FAVOR AND ABUNDANCE

1. As you navigate through your business, the Lord will open heavens for your sake and give you the favor you need in the eyes of people you meet everyday of your life in Jesus name. Amen.

2. You need an abundance of supernatural favor in your life and the Lord will send you uncommon supernatural favor from His Sanctuary in Jesus name. Amen.

3. Everything you lay your hands upon you will succeed in Jesus name. Amen.

4. Everything you lay your hands upon you will prosper in Jesus name. Amen.

5. No hand of the enemy will come near your life and business in Jesus name. Any hand of the enemy that tries to come and frustrate your life and business, I command it to dry up in Jesus name. Amen.

6. I decree uncommon blessings and financial abundance into your life right now in Jesus name. Amen.

7. I decree uncommon supernatural increase into your life and your family right now in Jesus name. Amen.

8. I decree that your business will succeed and expand to every part of the country and to other parts of the world in Jesus name. Amen.

9. I decree that people will seek you out and look for your products and services from all over the country and all over the world in Jesus name. Amen.

10. I decree the anointing of the Lord right now into your life and business in Jesus name. Amen

11. Every spirit of indebtedness and lack in your life and business that the enemy has programmed to embarrass you, I command the Holy ghost fire to destroy it right now in Jesus name. Amen.

SCRIPTURES FOR MEDITATION
Please meditate on these scriptures and pray with them.

"Kings of the earth and all peoples; Princes and all judges of the earth; Both young men and maidens; Old men and children. Let them praise the name of the Lord, For His name alone is exalted; His glory is above the earth and heaven. And He has exalted the horn of His people, The praise of all His saints-- Of the children of Israel, A people near to Him. Praise the Lord!" (Psalm 148:11-14)

"But my eyes are upon You, O God the Lord; In You I take refuge; Do not leave my soul destitute. Keep me from the snares they have laid for me, And from the traps of the workers of iniquity. Let the wicked fall into their own nets, While I escape safely." (Psalm 141:8-10)

*"Oh, give thanks to the Lord, for He is good! For His mercy endures forever.
Oh, give thanks to the God of gods! For His mercy endures forever.
Oh, give thanks to the Lord of lords! For His mercy endures forever:
To Him who alone does great wonders, For His mercy endures forever;
To Him who by wisdom made the heavens, For His mercy endures forever;
To Him who laid out the earth above the waters, For His mercy endures forever;"
(Psalm 136:1-6)*

*"Blessed is every one who fears the Lord, Who walks in His ways.
When you eat the labor of your hands, You shall be happy, and it shall be well with you."
(Psalm 128:1-2)*

"Let not the foot of pride come against me, And let not the hand of the wicked drive me away." (Psalm 36:11)

CHAPTER 10

RUNNING PROMOS & GIVING OF BONUSES

"Give, and it will be given to you: good measure, pressed down, shaken together, and running over will be put into your bosom. For with the same measure that you use, it will be measured back to you." (Luke 6:38)

"I have shown you in every way, by laboring like this, that you must support the weak. And remember the words of the Lord Jesus, that He said, 'It is more blessed to give than to receive.' " (Acts 20:35)

One of the easiest ways to connect with your customers and make them happy is to give them freebies. Everyone likes to be appreciated. Everyone likes to receive a gift. But your customers are special because they are the life wire of your business.

There is something so powerful about giving that many people don't know. Giving has a spiritual force behind it that rewards the giver sooner or later. Giving is a blessing to the giver but it should be done with good intentions.

It's so rewarding to give because it's an act of love and it should not only be done in your personal life but in your business as well. But here the aim is to gain you more customers and increase your sales because the more customers you have the more sales you will make.

So you should devise a strategy to give back to your customers in the form of special bonuses and attractive giveaways that will make you irresistible to them. It will be difficult for them to leave you and patronize your competitors because they know you will always appreciate them.

One of the ways to build trust and get loyal customers is to give them free items, free services and lots of bonuses. They value it so much but a lot of businesses do not know this. Although it's not easy to give freebies, but it's a sure marketing strategy to increase sales and retain your customers.

Tips On Running Promos & Giving Freebies

1. Give every customer who buys a certain quantity some kind of automatic discounts.

2. Ensure you run a promo for your business at regular intervals, especially at festive seasons when people spend a lot and more people will be in town, seeking for items to buy.

3. State it clearly in writing the bonuses and freebies available and the terms and conditions to qualify for them.

4. Ensure that what you're offering in your bonus package is unique and not obtainable elsewhere.

5. If you're rendering services, consider having various price points for the same service, but with discounts where possible.

6. Don't be too rigid in business if you want to go far. Be flexible and give consideration for negotiation. Make your goods or services to be negotiable where possible. This will make you not to lose certain customers who would want to strike a bargain with you.

7. If your business is about rendering services, consider giving free services to attract new clients who are yet to trust you and who have never bought your services before, to encourage them to patronize you. If they are satisfied with your services, they will spread the word about your business.

PRAYERS TO BRING GOOD CUSTOMERS

1. As you sow the seed of hard work and dedication in your business, the Lord will reward your efforts and bless the works of your hands abundantly in Jesus name. Amen.

3. The Lord will direct good customers to your business that will buy large quantities of your goods and services in Jesus name. Any bad customer that will cause you losses, I blind their eyes spiritually not to ever be able to locate you in Jesus name. Amen.

2. Any customer that will cause trouble for you, the Lord will not allow such customer to even know the direction of your shop or office in Jesus name. Amen.

3. Any customer who was sent as an agent of darkness to monitor and destabilise your business, the Lord will blind their eyes and ears spiritually not to even know your shop and I destroy their evil plans against your business in Jesus name. Amen.

4. Any customer that has been sent as an agent of darkness to cause trouble in your business in order to put you into indebtedness, by the authority in the Blood of Jesus Christ I destroy their evil plans right now in Jesus name. Amen.

5. Any customer that has been sent by Satan and his demons to come and collect any item in your shop for them to use it as a point of contact to destroy your business, by the authority in the Blood of Jesus Christ I destroy their evil plans right now in Jesus name. Amen.

6. Anybody in your family who is a monitoring spirit or an agent of Satan and who is not happy about your business and who is being used by Satan and his demons to obtain vital information about your business in order to do you evil or to cause the crashing of your business, by the authority in the Blood of Jesus Christ, I cancel all their evil plans right now in Jesus name. Amen.

7. I cover you and your family with the precious Blood of Jesus Christ. I decree supernatural abundance in your life that everything you do no matter how little you start will blossom and become big in Jesus name. Amen.

The peace of the Lord be with you in Jesus name. Amen.

SCRIPTURES FOR MEDITATION
Please read and meditate on the following scriptures.

"But this I say: He who sows sparingly will also reap sparingly, and he who sows bountifully will also reap bountifully. So let each one give as he purposes in his heart, not grudgingly or of necessity; for God loves a cheerful giver." *(2nd Corinthians 9:6-7)*

"Take heed that you do not do your charitable deeds before men, to be seen by them. Otherwise you have no reward from your Father in heaven. Therefore, when you do a charitable deed, do not sound a trumpet before you as the hypocrites do in the synagogues and in the streets, that they may have glory from men. Assuredly, I say to you, they have their reward. But when you do a charitable deed, do not let your left hand know what your right hand is doing, that your charitable deed may be in secret; and your Father who sees in secret will Himself reward you openly." *(Matthew 6:1-4)*

"Do not withhold good from those to whom it is due, When it is in the power of your hand to do so." *(Proverbs 3:27)*

"He who has pity on the poor lends to the Lord, And He will pay back what he has given." *(Proverbs 19:17)*

"But do not forget to do good and to share, for with such sacrifices God is well pleased." *(Hebrews 13:16)*

"He who gives to the poor will not lack, But he who hides his eyes will have many curses." *(Proverbs 28:27)*

"And my God shall supply all your need according to His riches in glory by Christ Jesus." *(Philippians 4:19)*

CHAPTER 11

PROPER COMMUNICATION WITH YOUR CUSTOMERS

"Let no corrupt word proceed out of your mouth, but what is good for necessary edification, that it may impart grace to the hearers." (Ephesians 4:29)

"Let your speech always be with grace, seasoned with salt, that you may know how you ought to answer each one." (Colossians 4:6)

"A soft answer turns away wrath, But a harsh word stirs up anger." (Proverbs 15:1)

In every aspect of life, communication is very important and this applies to your business as well. It can make a lot of difference when handled properly. Since communication is a two-way traffic, it must be done properly or else the essence will be lost.

Sometimes you may be trying to pass a message to your customers but they may not understand it because it's not properly communicated. So it's not enough to reach out to them, but do they understand your message?

Have you communicated it in the language they will understand? Have you studied them to know the best way to communicate your message to them that will make them understand you?

People are so diverse with different beliefs and cultures. One of the ways to get them to patronize you is to understand basic things about them and to communicate with them in the language they will understand and appreciate. You will achieve your aims faster this way.

People are usually conservative and skeptical about new things. You must realize that sometimes they have so many options to choose from and each seller is trying their best to convince them to buy from them.

So it can sometimes be very confusing for a customer to choose when presented with many options. That's why you must know how to clearly communicate with them in the best way they would understand and appreciate your message.

Many times it's not really the message you're trying to pass across, but how you pass the message matters. It can easily be misunderstood if not properly communicated. The essence of it can be lost and it will become a waste of time if you're not skilled in the art of business communication.

It does not matter the size of your business. Every business must ensure their channel of communication with their customers is open and reachable at all times

Tips On Sustaining Communication With Your Clients

1. Reach out to your clients and prospective clients from time to time. A lot of clients and prospective clients value this so much.

2. Follow-up prospective clients at regular intervals through phone calls, mails or Whatsapp chats.

3. Send them messages during festive periods to wish them well. This will make them know you care about them.

4. Don't harass your clients with too many phone calls. It can be a complete turn off for most people when you bother them too much with phone calls. Respect their privacy and call them only at reasonable intervals.

5. Proper and well monitored channels of communication can turn a prospective customer to a buying customer.

6. Address customer complaints promptly and don't keep them waiting endlessly to get an issue resolved. This can lead to resentment and frustration on the part of your customer and can make you lose such customer.

PRAYER FOR FINANCIAL FAVOR, OPEN HEAVENS AND FINANCIAL BREAKTHROUGH IN YOUR BUSINESS

1. I decree and declare by the authority in the word of the Lord in the book of Job 22:28 and by the authority in the Blood of Jesus Christ shed on the cross of Calvary, that from now on the Lord will give you the grace to be inspired with good business ideas that will move your business to the next level in Jesus name. Amen.

2. I decree that every good business idea you're inspired with, the Lord will send you the right people or team that will partner with you in order to execute it in Jesus name. Amen.

3. I decree continuous open heavens of financial favor in every aspect of your life and business in Jesus name. Amen.

4. I decree that even when there is financial hardship in your country or town, you will not see any financial hardship in your business and there will be permanent open heavens for your sake in Jesus name. Amen.

5. I decree that you shall never lack any good thing in your life in Jesus name. Amen.

6. I decree that you shall never lack money in your life in Jesus name. Amen

7. I decree that the money you need to expand your business, the Lord will give it to you in Jesus name. Amen.

8. I decree that the government will not close down your business in Jesus name. Amen.

9. I decree that no powers of darkness will come near your business in Jesus name. Amen.

10. I decree and declare by the authority in the Blood of Jesus Christ that any demonic powers that have been programmed to set you up in order to crash your business, I command the fire of the holy ghost to destroy their powers right now in Jesus name. Amen.

11. I decree uncommon financial favor and uncommon financial breakthrough into your business right now in Jesus name. Amen.

SCRIPTURES FOR MEDITATION

Please meditate on these scriptures and pray with them.

"My voice You shall hear in the morning, O Lord; In the morning I will direct it to You, And I will look up." *(Psalm 5:3)*

"Blessed is the man Who walks not in the counsel of the ungodly, Nor stands in the path of sinners, Nor sits in the seat of the scornful; But his delight is in the law of the Lord, And in His law he meditates day and night. He shall be like a tree Planted by the rivers of water, That brings forth its fruit in its season, Whose leaf also shall not wither; And whatever he does shall prosper." *(Psalm 1:1-3)*

"Lead me, O Lord, in Your righteousness because of my enemies; Make Your way straight before my face." *(Psalm 5:8)*

"The steps of a good man are ordered by the Lord, And He delights in his way. Though he fall, he shall not be utterly cast down; For the Lord upholds him with His hand." *(Psalm 37:23-24)*

"Surely goodness and mercy shall follow me All the days of my life; And I will dwell in the house of the Lord Forever." *(Psalm 23:6)*

"So then, my beloved brethren, let every man be swift to hear, slow to speak, slow to wrath; for the wrath of man does not produce the righteousness of God." *(James 1:19-20)*

"There is one who speaks like the piercings of a sword, But the tongue of the wise promotes health." *(Proverbs 12:18)*

"In the multitude of words sin is not lacking, But he who restrains his lips is wise." *(Proverbs 10:19)*

"And let us not grow weary while doing good, for in due season we shall reap if we do not lose heart. Therefore, as we have opportunity, let us do good to all, especially to those who are of the household of faith." *(Galatians 6:9-10)*

CHAPTER 12

WHY PATIENCE IS VITAL

"Rest in the Lord, and wait patiently for Him; Do not fret because of him who prospers in his way, Because of the man who brings wicked schemes to pass. Cease from anger, and forsake wrath; Do not fret--it only causes harm. For evildoers shall be cut off; But those who wait on the Lord, They shall inherit the earth. For yet a little while and the wicked shall be no more; Indeed, you will look carefully for his place, But it shall be no more." (Psalm 37:7-10)

Have you been so hard working, praying and fasting and waiting on the Lord to bless you but you're yet to see any improvement? Have you tried everything possible but yet to see any changes? Have you been so anxious about the financial situation in your business and you're on the verge of giving up?

The Lord Jesus loves you and He is calling you today as you read this. The Lord is telling you not to give up but to keep trying and He will soon answer your prayers. If you've tried everything possible and it didn't work or hasn't worked yet, then try patience. Try waiting continuously and never give up no matter the circumstances.

If you've tried everything you know about and it hasn't worked yet, then just hold on because very soon you will begin to see results and the Lord will open new doors of grace and opportunities for you.

You must never give up no matter the situation. You must never allow the enemy to confuse you and lie to you that the Lord cannot do it for you. Don't ever allow the lies of Satan and his demons to make you feel bad about your financial situation or about your life.

The Bible says everything works together for good for those that believe. You must know that delay is not denial. Sometimes it may come to test your faith or to help in building your life and resistance, so that when eventually the fruits of your labor begin to manifest, you will know how to manage it.

If you want to succeed in business, you must be patient because not everything you want will come to you when you desire it.

You must learn to endure a lot of challenges in your business and wait upon the Lord to do it for you at the right time. The right time for God to bless you is the best time for you, not your own time, but God's own time.

If you insist on not waiting for God's time and you rush it, it can be very dangerous for your life because you can miss God's appointed blessing for you. You can miss a lot of favors and opportunities which God has programmed for you.

Learn to wait for God's time if you've tried everything possible and it didn't work. There's a reason why it's happening to you. There's a reason why the Lord made it happen to you. For there's nothing that happens on the surface of this earth that the Lord is not aware of. Nothing just happens, everything happens for a reason.

Patience is key in business. Not everyone who contacts you will patronize you immediately, some will take their time. If you attend to them well when they come to inquire about your business and offers, they will come back and patronize you later in the future. They will always remember how nice you were to them or how good your staff treated them and they will come back.

Be patient. Wait for your time and don't rush your life or follow people who are serving Satan to think that things happen without a process.

There are processes, protocols and procedures involved in the things of God and your own process may not be the same with that of another person. So wait for God to unveil your own process to you and wait till He tells you it's time.

When it's God's time for your life, no man can stop it, but if you rush your life you will miss God's agenda for you and before you realize it, it would have been too late.

This is why many people have missed their glorious destinies because they were not patient enough to wait for their time. They were misled by Satan and his demons into thinking that they could get it by cutting corners or by cheating or by worshipping Satan.

So they sold their souls to Satan in exchange for wealth but today they are regretting it and wishing they could turn back the hands of time.

They are wishing they never involved themselves in such a mess but alas it's already too late because they've been lied to and they believed the lie of Satan and his demonic agents whose sole aim is to steal, to kill and to destroy. Beware!

If you keep believing and being faithful to the Lord, He will never let you down. He will be with you and your business. He will lift you up at the right time.

So don't give up, the Lord is your strength.

The peace of the Lord be with you in Jesus name. Amen.

PRAYERS TO BREAK DEMONIC SPELLS, DEMONIC YOKES AND DEMONIC CURSES OVER YOUR BUSINESS & FINANCES

1. By the authority in the Blood of Jesus Christ shed on the cross of Calvary, I break every demonic spell or curse upon your business and upon your finances right now in Jesus name. Amen.

2. By the power of the holy ghost I break any curse of the enemy upon your finances as a result of any mistake you've made in the past in Jesus name. Amen.

3. By the authority in the Blood of Jesus Christ shed on the cross of Calvary, I set you free from all witchcraft powers, from all ancestral curses, from all ancestral powers, from all curses from any human being living or dead, I set you free right now in Jesus name. Amen.

4. I decree and declare that you will never be put to shame in Jesus name. Amen.

5. Every plot of the enemy to cause you financial embarrassment, I cancel it right now in Jesus name. Amen.

6. I decree and declare a complete turn around in your business and in your finances in Jesus name. Amen.

SCRIPTURES FOR MEDITATION

Please meditate on these scriptures and pray with them.

"Be anxious for nothing, but in everything by prayer and supplication, with thanksgiving, let your requests be made known to God; and the peace of God, which surpasses all understanding, will guard your hearts and minds through Christ Jesus." (Philippians 4:6-7)

"But those who wait on the Lord Shall renew their strength; They shall mount up with wings like eagles, They shall run and not be weary, They shall walk and not faint." (Isaiah 40:31)

"The end of a thing is better than its beginning; The patient in spirit is better than the proud in spirit. Do not hasten in your spirit to be angry, For anger rests in the bosom of fools." (Ecclesiastes 7:8-9)

"For you have need of endurance, so that after you have done the will of God, you may receive the promise:" (Hebrews 10:36)

"Therefore be patient, brethren, until the coming of the Lord. See how the farmer waits for the precious fruit of the earth, waiting patiently for it until it receives the early and latter rain. You also be patient. Establish your hearts, for the coming of the Lord is at hand." (James 5:7-8)

"I waited patiently for the Lord; And He inclined to me, And heard my cry. He also brought me up out of a horrible pit, Out of the miry clay, And set my feet upon a rock, And established my steps. He has put a new song in my mouth-- Praise to our God; Many will see it and fear, And will trust in the Lord." (Psalm 40:1-3)

"Wait on the Lord; Be of good courage, And He shall strengthen your heart; Wait, I say, on the Lord!" (Psalm 27:14)

CHAPTER 13

WHY YOU NEED A SOCIAL MEDIA MANAGER

"Unless the Lord builds the house, They labor in vain who build it; Unless the Lord guards the city, The watchman stays awake in vain. It is vain for you to rise up early, To sit up late, To eat the bread of sorrows; For so He gives His beloved sleep." (Psalm 127: 1-2)

If you want to take your business to greater heights, you need a social media manager to manage all your business pages on several social media platforms.

A social media manager can be a person or a team of persons whom you assign the role to oversee the running of your social media pages.

A social media manager is very important in your business if you're serious about making a strong impact on the social media circles.

The more presence you have on social media, the more people know your business and the more income you will make because people will only buy from those they know.

STRATEGIES FOR SOCIAL MEDIA MANAGEMENT

As a business owner, you have to evolve a strategy for your social media management.

You must have a team to manage your social media profiles, pages and handle your social media campaigns and adverts.

If you have a social media manager or social media team, then you need to assign them with their responsibilities, which have to be clearly spelt out in written form before engaging your team with their tasks.

Your social media manager must be well acquainted with this role in order to deliver on his responsibilities.

He must be able to deliver good returns on investment on your promotion and advertising campaigns.

The following are the responsibilities of your social media manager.

RESPONSIBILITIES OF SOCIAL MEDIA MANAGER

1. Management Of Social Media Handles And Pages: Your social media manager must devise a viable plan on how to manage your business pages on all social media platforms.

He must be creative, with great ideas and concepts on how to run your social media pages for serious engagement with your customers and prospects.

He must be familiar with how different social media platforms work, their rules and how to harness the immense potential of social media to promote your business and acquire new clients on an ongoing basis.

He must know how best to utilize several social media networks such as Facebook, Twitter, Instagram, Nairaland, Whatsapp, etc, to promote your business to the world and acquire more clients.

2. Creating Content: Your social media manager must create relevant content that will appeal to your audience. He must study the trend and create what will resonate with the current trend and your brand at the same time.

It must be something that will pass a message to the audience and connect with your brand and make a lasting impact on your audience.

He must also draft promotion ads for your business or company, which should suit your marketing goals and objectives.

3. Regular Posting And Updating Of Content On Social Media Pages: Your social media team must devise a strategic plan to post engaging content on all your social media pages on a regular basis for constant engagement with your clients.

One important thing about social media is to be consistent. The more consistent you are on social media with your business, the more seriously people will take your business. If you're always posting relevant information or content, the more people will notice you on social media.

4. Engagement With Your Audience On Social Media: The people on social media are curious to know more about your business. They will ask relevant questions about what you do or offer. They need answers and someone to attend to them before they can make a decision whether to patronize you or not.

Your social media manager must know how to properly engage with your customers and business prospects and convert them to paying customers.

5. Market Research: Another important thing your social media manager must do is to properly research the market for trending issues, concepts and also research about your competitors to obtain relevant information about them which will help your business.

You must use the information obtained to advance your marketing objective. You must be constantly improving on your business brand and to do this, you need to have relevant information on what you're doing right or wrong. You must know what areas you need to improve upon.

6. Creating & Implementing Ad Campaigns: Another vital role your social media manager should play is to create and implement ad campaigns and promotion plans for your business brand.

Different social media platforms should have different ad campaign templates and timing for your products or services.

Proper segmentation with segregated time placement of each ad will make you able to track the performance of each ad campaign.

This is important especially if you're just starting out with advertising to enable you understand the intricacies involved in running ads on each platform.

7. Copywriting: Generating ideas, planning and writing text ads about your business brand and posting on your social media pages is another area where your social media manager should focus on.

Text ads are very powerful in conveying the message of your brand to your customers and prospects. For more engagement, text ads about your business or brand should be written and posted on social media platforms such as Nairaland, Instagram, Facebook, Twitter and whatsapp broadcast to reach millions of people.

8. Posting Banner Ads: Another important aspect of promotion which your social media manager should handle is to regularly post well crafted banner ads on social media platforms to generate comments and engagement.

A lot of people even prefer banner ads to text ads. People can easily remember a banner or picture ad more than a text ad.

Beautifully designed banner ads with pictures of your products or services should be regularly posted on your social media platforms and also shared on other networks for wider reach.

9. General Branding: Your social media manager must generate ideas on how to properly brand your business to project the right image of the products or services you offer to the world.

The marketing and promotion of your business must be targeted at not just getting new customers regularly but also on retaining old customers and expanding your business to other towns and cities.

MY PRAYERS FOR YOU OVER YOUR EMPLOYEES

1. Any employee that the enemy will use to make your business crumble, by the power of the holy ghost I destroy all their evil plans against your business right now in Jesus name. Amen.

2. I decree that any employee that wants to steal your money or property in order to crumble your business, their eyes will be blinded spiritually not to even see your money or property in Jesus name. Amen.

3. I decree that any staff who has vowed to be a stumbling block to your business, he or she will be exposed in Jesus name. Amen.

4. Any employee who is being used as an agent of darkness as a monitoring spirit to monitor your business and give information to Satan and his demons, I decree that such staff will be exposed and your business will be set free in Jesus name. Amen.

5. May the Lord grant you the grace to discern the kind of staff you should employ and the type you should not employ in Jesus name. Amen.

6. May the Lord open your spiritual eyes during the employment process to know the kind of staff that fit perfectly into your business and to know those that will take your business higher in Jesus name. Amen.

7. Any staff who will be used by the enemy to leak your secrets or your company secrets to your competitors, I decree that such staff will be exposed in Jesus name. Amen.

8. Any employee that the enemy will use to put you into trouble, I decree that he or she will be exposed before they execute their evil plans and I destroy all their evil plots against your business in Jesus name. Amen.

SCRIPTURES FOR MEDITATION

Please meditate on these scriptures and pray with them.

"'You shall not cheat your neighbor, nor rob him. The wages of him who is hired shall not remain with you all night until morning." (Leviticus 19:13)

"Servants, be submissive to your masters with all fear, not only to the good and gentle, but also to the harsh. For this is commendable, if because of conscience toward God one endures grief, suffering wrongfully." (1st Peter 2:18-19)

"Bondservants, obey in all things your masters according to the flesh, not with eyeservice, as menpleasers, but in sincerity of heart, fearing God. And whatever you do, do it heartily, as to the Lord and not to men, knowing that from the Lord you will receive the reward of the inheritance; for you serve the Lord Christ. But he who does wrong will be repaid for what he has done, and there is no partiality." (Colossians 3:22-25)

"Exhort bondservants to be obedient to their own masters, to be well pleasing in all things, not answering back, not pilfering, but showing all good fidelity, that they may adorn the doctrine of God our Savior in all things." (Titus 2:9-10)

"Let as many bondservants as are under the yoke count their own masters worthy of all honor, so that the name of God and His doctrine may not be blasphemed. And those who have believing masters, let them not despise them because they are brethren, but rather serve them because those who are benefited are believers and beloved. Teach and exhort these things." (1st Timothy 6:1-2)

"Therefore, my beloved brethren, be steadfast, immovable, always abounding in the work of the Lord, knowing that your labor is not in vain in the Lord." (1st Corinthians 15:58)

CHAPTER 14

EPILOGUE: YOUR BUSINESS WILL SUCCEED

"And you shall remember the Lord your God, for it is He who gives you power to get wealth, that He may establish His covenant which He swore to your fathers, as it is this day." (Deuteronomy 8:18)

Most big businesses started small, so your business too can become a big brand. Do you believe this?

It starts from your knowledge and understanding of the potentials in your business.

It starts from your ability to harness your potentials and strengths to move your business to greater heights.

If the big brands did it, you too can do it. If the big brands could become big, you too can become big with your business.

Your own business too can become a big brand if you believe and work towards it.

Yes you can.

All things are possible to those who believe.

"Jesus said to him, "If you can believe, all things are possible to him who believes.' " (Mark 9:23)

With proper planning and execution, you can take your business to any level you desire.

Many of the great brands actually started with one person, sometimes at the corner of a room, sometimes on a single computer.

So if you believe you can succeed with your business and you work earnestly towards it, you will achieve your dreams.

All things work together for good to those who believe.

"And we know that all things work together for good to those who love God, to those who are the called according to His purpose. For whom He foreknew, He also predestined to be conformed to the image of His Son, that He might be the firstborn among many brethren. Moreover whom He predestined, these He also called; whom He called, these He also justified; and whom He justified, these He also glorified." (Romans 8:28-30)

DELIVERANCE & BREAKTHROUGH PRAYERS FOR YOUR BUSINESS

I decree by the authority in the Blood of Jesus Christ shed on the cross of Calvary that your business will succeed and prosper in Jesus name. Amen.

By the authority in the Blood of Jesus Christ shed on the cross of Calvary, I break every yoke of the enemy against your life and against your business in Jesus name.

I decree that everything you lay your hands upon will prosper.

I cover your business with the Blood of Jesus Christ. I cover your finances with the Blood of Jesus Christ.

I decree that no weapon formed against you shall prosper in Jesus name.

I bless the works of your hands in Jesus name.

You will live to fulfill your glory in Jesus name.

I decree uncommon supernatural favor into your life right now in Jesus name.

I decree uncommon financial favor into your life right now in Jesus name.

I decree uncommon success into your life right now in Jesus name.

I decree uncommon financial breakthrough into your life right now in Jesus name.

I decree by the authority in the Blood of Jesus Christ shed on the cross of Calvary that you will never lack any good thing in your life in Jesus name.

I decree by the authority in the Blood of Jesus Christ shed on the cross of Calvary that you will never lack money in your life in Jesus name.

The peace of the Lord be with you in Jesus name. Amen.

God bless you.

CHAPTER 15

WHAT'S YOUR HOPE OF ETERNITY?

Brethren,

What is your hope of eternal life? What is your hope in the kingdom of our Lord?

If this world ends today, where will you be? For what shall it profit a man if he gains the whole world but loses his soul in hell? What shall it profit you if you have all the possessions in the world but lose your life at the end of the world?

Are you born again? The scriptures tell us that anyone who is not born again cannot enter the kingdom of God.

"Jesus answered and said to him, "Most assuredly, I say to you, unless one is born again, he cannot see the kingdom of God." (John 3:3)

If this world ends right now as you read this, where will you go? Is your name written in the book of life?

If you've not yet given your life to Christ today, please do so now. Our Lord Jesus Christ loves you so much and cares so much about you. He wants you to know Him and to worship the Lord in truth and in sincerity. He is waiting for you with open arms to receive you into His Kingdom.

He sacrificed His own life and died for us on the cross of Calvary and shed His Precious Blood to save us from eternal death.

He was crucified on the cross of Calvary to save you and me from eternal death. He died and resurrected on the third day and ascended to heaven where He sits at the right hand of the Father.

If you have not yet given your life to Christ, please kindly say this short prayer with me. Please kindly say it aloud:

Lord Jesus, I confess my sins to you. I repent of all my sins. I surrender my life to You from today and I want You to take charge of my life and touch me with Your mighty power. I acknowledge that You were crucified for my sins and You died and resurrected on the third day and ascended to heaven. Forgive my sins Lord and save my life. Amen.

If you have said that short prayer, then congratulations!

I would like to hear from you if you've been blessed by this message. I would like to hear your story and how the Lord touched your life or any other issues you may have.

I would like to hear your testimony for I know the Lord will touch your life positively.

Keep abiding in faith in the Lord.

Please drop me a line below.

Send me a mail via tayodemola@gmail.com

God bless you.

CHAPTER 16

25 MIRACULOUS PSALMS

The following are 25 miraculous Psalms you can always use for your prayers. As long as you believe, they will work for you.

You can use them for prayers for healing, for deliverance, for business success, for breakthrough prayers, for those seeking for the fruit of the womb, for treating various ailments and diseases, for prayers against spiritual attacks from the enemy and spiritual warfare against the kingdom of darkness, etc.

I have reproduced each Psalm below. You can read and pray them anytime of the day but the most potent and effective time to use them in prayers is at night between the hours of 11pm to 6am, especially between 12am and 4am.

All Scriptures were taken from the New King James Version of the Holy Bible.

PSALM 23
THE LORD THE SHEPHERD OF HIS PEOPLE

(NB: This Psalm is a multi purpose Psalm which can be used to solve various issues depending on how the Holy Spirit leads you. It has universal applications. It's a Psalm you should memorize and recite it everyday. It's a very powerful Psalm.)

A Psalm of David.

1 The Lord is my shepherd; I shall not want.

2 He makes me to lie down in green pastures;
He leads me beside the still waters.

3 He restores my soul; He leads me in the paths of righteousness For His name's sake.

4 Yea, though I walk through the valley of the shadow of death, I will fear no evil; For You are with me;
Your rod and Your staff, they comfort me.

5 You prepare a table before me in the presence of my enemies;
You anoint my head with oil;
My cup runs over.

6 Surely goodness and mercy shall follow me
All the days of my life;
And I will dwell in the house of the Lord
Forever.

PSALM 91
ABIDING IN THE SHADOW OF THE ALMIGHTY

(NB: This Psalm can be used for all purposes, especially for spiritual protection and spiritual warfare. Read this Psalm every night before going to bed and you will never have any bad dreams, spiritual attacks or nightmares. It's a very powerful Psalm for spiritual warfare. It can also be used by soldiers or military men going to the war front, for protection against bullet wounds or injuries. It can also be used by any other person for protection against bullet or stray bullet. If you read this Psalm everyday, you'll be able to withstand spiritual battles.)

1 He who dwells in the secret place of the Most High Shall abide under the shadow of the Almighty.

2 I will say of the Lord, "He is my refuge and my fortress;
My God, in Him I will trust."

3 Surely He shall deliver you from the snare of the fowler
And from the perilous pestilence.

4 He shall cover you with His feathers,
And under His wings you shall take refuge;
His truth shall be your shield and buckler.

5 You shall not be afraid of the terror by night,
Nor of the arrow that flies by day,

6 Nor of the pestilence that walks in darkness,
Nor of the destruction that lays waste at noonday.

7 A thousand may fall at your side,
And ten thousand at your right hand;
But it shall not come near you.

8 Only with your eyes shall you look,
And see the reward of the wicked.

9 Because you have made the Lord, who is my refuge, Even the Most High, your dwelling place,

10 No evil shall befall you,
Nor shall any plague come near your dwelling;

11 For He shall give His angels charge over you,
To keep you in all your ways.

12 In their hands they shall bear you up,
Lest you dash your foot against a stone.

13 You shall tread upon the lion and the cobra,

The young lion and the serpent you shall trample underfoot.

14 "Because he has set his love upon Me, therefore I will deliver him;
I will set him on high, because he has known My name.

15 He shall call upon Me, and I will answer him;
I will be with him in trouble;
I will deliver him and honor him.

16 With long life I will satisfy him,
And show him My salvation."

PSALM 24
THE KING OF GLORY
(NB: This Psalm can be used for all purposes.)

A Psalm of David.

1 The earth is the Lord's, and all its fullness,
The world and those who dwell therein.

2 For He has founded it upon the seas,
And established it upon the waters.

3 Who may ascend into the hill of the Lord?
Or who may stand in His holy place?

4 He who has clean hands and a pure heart,
Who has not lifted up his soul to an idol,
Nor sworn deceitfully.

5 He shall receive blessing from the Lord,
And righteousness from the God of his salvation.

6 This is Jacob, the generation of those who seek Him, Who seek Your face. Selah

7 Lift up your heads, O you gates!
And be lifted up, you everlasting doors!
And the King of glory shall come in.

8 Who is this King of glory?
The Lord strong and mighty,
The Lord mighty in battle.

9 Lift up your heads, O you gates!
Lift up, you everlasting doors!
And the King of glory shall come in.

10 Who is this King of glory?
The Lord of hosts,
He is the King of glory.
Selah

PSALM 121
THE LORD IS MY KEEPER

(NB: Use this Psalm for all purposes depending on how the Holy Spirit leads you. It's particularly good to read it early in the morning before going out.)

A Song of Ascents.

1 I will lift up my eyes to the hills--
From whence comes my help?

2 My help comes from the Lord,
Who made heaven and earth.

3 He will not allow your foot to be moved;
He who keeps you will not slumber.

4 Behold, He who keeps Israel
Shall neither slumber nor sleep.

5 The Lord is your keeper;
The Lord is your shade at your right hand.

6 The sun shall not strike you by day,
Nor the moon by night.

7 The Lord shall preserve you from all evil;
He shall preserve your soul.

8 The Lord shall preserve your going out and your coming in
From this time forth, and even forevermore.

PSALM 1
THE RIGHTEOUS AND THE UNGODLY

(NB: Read this Psalm and pray with it for success in business, financial breakthrough, contract, for those seeking employment, for fruit of the womb, for breaking of yokes, for spiritual warfare, etc.)

1 Blessed is the man
Who walks not in the counsel of the ungodly,
Nor stands in the path of sinners,
Nor sits in the seat of the scornful;

2 But his delight is in the law of the Lord,
And in His law he meditates day and night.

3 He shall be like a tree
Planted by the rivers of water, That brings forth its fruit in its season, Whose leaf also shall not wither; And whatever he does shall prosper.

4 The ungodly are not so, But are like the chaff which the wind drives away.

5 Therefore the ungodly shall not stand in the judgment, Nor sinners in the congregation of the righteous.

6 For the Lord knows the way of the righteous,
But the way of the ungodly shall perish.

PSALM 51
A PRAYER FOR CLEANSING

(NB: This Psalm can be used for all purposes. It's good to read this Psalm aloud before or after offering your prayers. It's one of those Psalms to be read on a daily basis. It's also a Psalm to be read for genuine repentance and for forgiveness of sins. It can also be used by women for cleansing after menstruation.)

To the Chief Musician. A Psalm of David when Nathan the prophet went to him, after he had gone in to Bathsheba.

1 Have mercy upon me, O God,
According to Your lovingkindness;
According to the multitude of Your tender mercies,
Blot out my transgressions.

2 Wash me thoroughly from my iniquity,
And cleanse me from my sin.

3 For I acknowledge my transgressions,
And my sin is always before me.

4 Against You, You only, have I sinned,
And done this evil in Your sight--
That You may be found just when You speak,
And blameless when You judge.

5 Behold, I was brought forth in iniquity,
And in sin my mother conceived me.

6 Behold, You desire truth in the inward parts,
And in the hidden part
You will make me to know wisdom.

7 Purge me with hyssop, and I shall be clean;
Wash me, and I shall be whiter than snow.

8 Make me hear joy and gladness,
That the bones You have broken may rejoice.

9 Hide Your face from my sins,
And blot out all my iniquities.

10 Create in me a clean heart, O God,
And renew a steadfast spirit within me.

11 Do not cast me away from Your presence,
And do not take Your Holy Spirit from me.

12 Restore to me the joy of Your salvation,
And uphold me by Your generous Spirit.

13 Then I will teach transgressors Your ways,
And sinners shall be converted to You.

14 Deliver me from the guilt of bloodshed, O God,
The God of my salvation,
And my tongue shall sing aloud of Your righteousness.

15 O Lord, open my lips,
And my mouth shall show forth Your praise.

16 For You do not desire sacrifice,
or else I would give it;
You do not delight in burnt offering.

17 The sacrifices of God are a broken spirit,
A broken and a contrite heart--
These, O God, You will not despise.

18 Do good in Your good pleasure to Zion;
Build the walls of Jerusalem.

19 Then You shall be pleased with the sacrifices of righteousness,
With burnt offering and whole burnt offering;
Then they shall offer bulls on Your altar.

PSALM 102
A CRY IN DISTRESS

A Prayer of the afflicted, when he is overwhelmed and pours out his complaint before the Lord.

1   Hear my prayer, O Lord,
And let my cry come to You.

2 Do not hide Your face from me in the day of my trouble;
Incline Your ear to me;
In the day that I call, answer me speedily.

3 For my days are consumed like smoke,
And my bones are burned like a hearth.

4 My heart is stricken and withered like grass,
So that I forget to eat my bread.

5 Because of the sound of my groaning
My bones cling to my skin.

6 I am like a pelican of the wilderness;
I am like an owl of the desert.

7 I lie awake,
And am like a sparrow alone on the housetop.

8 My enemies reproach me all day long,
Those who deride me swear an oath against me.

9 For I have eaten ashes like bread,
And mingled my drink with weeping,

10 Because of Your indignation and Your wrath;
For You have lifted me up and cast me away.

11 My days are like a shadow that lengthens,
And I wither away like grass.

12 But You, O Lord, shall endure forever,
And the remembrance of Your name to all generations.

13 You will arise and have mercy on Zion;
For the time to favor her, Yes, the set time, has come.

14 For Your servants take pleasure in her stones,
And show favor to her dust.

15 So the nations shall fear the name of the Lord,
And all the kings of the earth Your glory.

16 For the Lord shall build up Zion; He shall appear in His glory.

17 He shall regard the prayer of the destitute,
And shall not despise their prayer.

18 This will be written for the generation to come,
That a people yet to be created may praise the Lord.

19 For He looked down from the height of His sanctuary; From heaven the Lord viewed the earth,

20 To hear the groaning of the prisoner,
To release those appointed to death,

21 To declare the name of the Lord in Zion,
And His praise in Jerusalem,

22 When the peoples are gathered together,
And the kingdoms, to serve the Lord.

23 He weakened my strength in the way;
He shortened my days.

24 I said, "O my God,
Do not take me away in the midst of my days;
Your years are throughout all generations.

25 Of old You laid the foundation of the earth,
And the heavens are the work of Your hands.

26 They will perish, but You will endure;
Yes, they will all grow old like a garment;
Like a cloak You will change them,
And they will be changed.

27 But You are the same,
And Your years will have no end.

28 The children of Your servants will continue,
And their descendants will be established before You."

PSALM 145
PRAISE FOR THE LORD'S GOODNESS AND POWER

A Praise of David.

1 I will extol You, my God, O King;

And I will bless Your name forever and ever.

2 Every day I will bless You,
And I will praise Your name forever and ever.

3 Great is the Lord, and greatly to be praised;
And His greatness is unsearchable.

4 One generation shall praise Your works to another, And shall declare Your mighty acts.

5 I will meditate on the glorious splendor of Your majesty,
And on Your wondrous works.

6 Men shall speak of the might of Your awesome acts, And I will declare Your greatness.

7 They shall utter the memory of Your great goodness, And shall sing of Your righteousness.

8 The Lord is gracious and full of compassion,
Slow to anger and great in mercy.

9 The Lord is good to all,
And His tender mercies are over all His works.

10 All Your works shall praise You, O Lord,
And Your saints shall bless You.

11 They shall speak of the glory of Your kingdom,
And talk of Your power,

12 To make known to the sons of men His mighty acts, And the glorious majesty of His kingdom.

13 Your kingdom is an everlasting kingdom,
And Your dominion endures throughout all generations.

14 The Lord upholds all who fall,
And raises up all who are bowed down.

15 The eyes of all look expectantly to You,
And You give them their food in due season.

16 You open Your hand
And satisfy the desire of every living thing.

17 The Lord is righteous in all His ways,
Gracious in all His works.

18 The Lord is near to all who call upon Him,
To all who call upon Him in truth.

19 He will fulfill the desire of those who fear Him; He also will hear their cry and save them.

20 The Lord preserves all who love Him,
But all the wicked He will destroy.

21 My mouth shall speak the praise of the Lord,
And all flesh shall bless His holy name
Forever and ever.

PSALM 147
PRAISE FOR THE LORD'S FAVOR TO JERUSALEM

1 Praise the Lord!
For it is good to sing praises to our God;
For it is pleasant, and praise is beautiful.

2 The Lord builds up Jerusalem;
He gathers together the outcasts of Israel.

3 He heals the brokenhearted
And binds up their wounds.

4 He counts the number of the stars;
He calls them all by name.

5 Great is our Lord, and mighty in power;
His understanding is infinite.

6 The Lord lifts up the humble;
He casts the wicked down to the ground.

7 Sing to the Lord with thanksgiving;
Sing praises on the harp to our God,

8 Who covers the heavens with clouds,
Who prepares rain for the earth,
Who makes grass to grow on the mountains.

9 He gives to the beast its food,
And to the young ravens that cry.

10 He does not delight in the strength of the horse;
He takes no pleasure in the legs of a man.

11 The Lord takes pleasure in those who fear Him,
In those who hope in His mercy.

   12 Praise the Lord, O Jerusalem!
Praise your God, O Zion!

13 For He has strengthened the bars of your gates;
He has blessed your children within you.

14 He makes peace in your borders,
And fills you with the finest wheat.

15 He sends out His command to the earth;
His word runs very swiftly.

16 He gives snow like wool;
He scatters the frost like ashes;

17 He casts out His hail like morsels;
Who can stand before His cold?

18 He sends out His word and melts them;
He causes His wind to blow, and the waters flow.

19 He declares His word to Jacob,
His statutes and His judgments to Israel.

20 He has not dealt thus with any nation;
And as for His judgments, they have not known them. Praise the Lord!

PSALM 35
A PRAYER FOR RESCUE FROM ENEMIES

(NB: This Psalm can be used for spiritual warfare against spiritual attacks or any form of spiritual warfare.)

A Psalm of David.

1 Plead my cause, O Lord, with those who strive with me;
Fight against those who fight against me.

2 Take hold of shield and buckler,
And stand up for my help.

3 Also draw out the spear,
And stop those who pursue me.
Say to my soul, "I am your salvation."

4 Let those be put to shame and brought to dishonor
Who seek after my life;
Let those be turned back and brought to confusion
Who plot my hurt.

5 Let them be like chaff before the wind,
And let the angel of the Lord chase them.

6 Let their way be dark and slippery,
And let the angel of the Lord pursue them.

7 For without cause they have hidden their net for me in a pit,
Which they have dug without cause for my life.

8 Let destruction come upon him unexpectedly,
And let his net that he has hidden catch himself;
Into that very destruction let him fall.

9 And my soul shall be joyful in the Lord;
It shall rejoice in His salvation.

10 All my bones shall say,
"Lord, who is like You,
Delivering the poor from him who is too strong for him, Yes, the poor and the needy from him who plunders him?"

11 Fierce witnesses rise up;
They ask me things that I do not know.

12 They reward me evil for good,
To the sorrow of my soul.

13 But as for me, when they were sick,
My clothing was sackcloth;
I humbled myself with fasting;
And my prayer would return to my own heart.

14 I paced about as though he were my friend or brother;
I bowed down heavily,
as one who mourns for his mother.

15 But in my adversity they rejoiced
And gathered together;
Attackers gathered against me,
And I did not know it;
They tore at me and did not cease;

16 With ungodly mockers at feasts
They gnashed at me with their teeth.

17 Lord, how long will You look on?
Rescue me from their destructions,
My precious life from the lions.

18 I will give You thanks in the great assembly;
I will praise You among many people.

19 Let them not rejoice over me who are
wrongfully my enemies;
Nor let them wink with the eye who hate
me without a cause.

20 For they do not speak peace,
But they devise deceitful matters
Against the quiet ones in the land.

21 They also opened their mouth wide against me,
And said, "Aha, aha!
Our eyes have seen it."

22 This You have seen, O Lord;
Do not keep silence.
O Lord, do not be far from me.

23 Stir up Yourself, and awake to my vindication,
To my cause, my God and my Lord.

24 Vindicate me, O Lord my God,
according to Your righteousness;
And let them not rejoice over me.

25 Let them not say in their hearts,
"Ah, so we would have it!"
Let them not say,
"We have swallowed him up."

26 Let them be ashamed and brought to mutual confusion
Who rejoice at my hurt;
Let them be clothed with shame and dishonor
Who exalt themselves against me.

27 Let them shout for joy and be glad,
Who favor my righteous cause;
And let them say continually,
"Let the Lord be magnified,
Who has pleasure in the prosperity of His servant."

28 And my tongue shall speak of Your righteousness And of Your praise all the day long.

PSALM 109
A CRY FOR VENGEANCE

(NB: This Psalm is for spiritual warfare)

To the Chief Musician. A Psalm of David.

1 Do not keep silent,
O God of my praise!

2 For the mouth of the wicked and the mouth of the deceitful
Have opened against me;
They have spoken against me with a lying tongue.

3 They have also surrounded me
with words of hatred,
And fought against me without a cause.

4 In return for my love they are my accusers,
But I give myself to prayer.

5 Thus they have rewarded me evil for good,
And hatred for my love.

6 Set a wicked man over him,
And let an accuser stand at his right hand.

7 When he is judged, let him be found guilty,
And let his prayer become sin.

8 Let his days be few,
And let another take his office.

9 Let his children be fatherless,
And his wife a widow.

10 Let his children continually be vagabonds,
and beg;
Let them seek their bread also from their
desolate places.

11 Let the creditor seize all that he has,
And let strangers plunder his labor.

12 Let there be none to extend mercy to him,
Nor let there be any to favor his fatherless children.

13 Let his posterity be cut off,
And in the generation following let their name be blotted out.

14 Let the iniquity of his fathers be
remembered before the Lord,
And let not the sin of his mother be blotted out.

15 Let them be continually before the Lord,
That He may cut off the memory of them from the earth;

16 Because he did not remember to show mercy,
But persecuted the poor and needy man,
That he might even slay the broken in heart.

17 As he loved cursing, so let it come to him;
As he did not delight in blessing,
so let it be far from him.

18 As he clothed himself with cursing as with his garment,
So let it enter his body like water,
And like oil into his bones.

19 Let it be to him like the garment which covers him, And for a belt with which he girds himself continually.

20 Let this be the Lord's reward to my accusers,
And to those who speak evil against my person.

21 But You, O God the Lord,
Deal with me for Your name's sake;
Because Your mercy is good, deliver me.

22 For I am poor and needy,
And my heart is wounded within me.
23 I am gone like a shadow when it lengthens;
I am shaken off like a locust.

24 My knees are weak through fasting,
And my flesh is feeble from lack of fatness.

25 I also have become a reproach to them;
When they look at me, they shake their heads.

26 Help me, O Lord my God!
Oh, save me according to Your mercy,

27 That they may know that this is Your hand--
That You, Lord, have done it!

28 Let them curse, but You bless;
When they arise, let them be ashamed,
But let Your servant rejoice.

29 Let my accusers be clothed with shame,
And let them cover themselves with their own disgrace as with a mantle.

30 I will greatly praise the Lord with my mouth;
Yes, I will praise Him among the multitude.

31 For He shall stand at the right hand of the poor,
To save him from those who condemn him.

PSALM 31
A PROFESSION OF TRUST

(NB: This Psalm can be used for all purposes.)

To the Chief Musician. A Psalm of David.

1   In You, O Lord, I put my trust;
Let me never be ashamed;
Deliver me in Your righteousness.

2 Bow down Your ear to me,
Deliver me speedily;
Be my rock of refuge,
A fortress of defense to save me.

3 For You are my rock and my fortress;
Therefore, for Your name's sake,
Lead me and guide me.

4 Pull me out of the net which they have secretly laid for me,
For You are my strength.

5 Into Your hand I commit my spirit;
You have redeemed me, O Lord God of truth.

6 I have hated those who regard useless idols;
But I trust in the Lord.

7 I will be glad and rejoice in Your mercy,
For You have considered my trouble;
You have known my soul in adversities,

8 And have not shut me up into the hand of
the enemy;
You have set my feet in a wide place.

9 Have mercy on me, O Lord, for I am in trouble;
My eye wastes away with grief,
Yes, my soul and my body!

10 For my life is spent with grief,
And my years with sighing;
My strength fails because of my iniquity,
And my bones waste away.

11 I am a reproach among all my enemies,

But especially among my neighbors,
And am repulsive to my acquaintances;
Those who see me outside flee from me.

12 I am forgotten like a dead man, out of mind;
I am like a broken vessel.

13 For I hear the slander of many;
Fear is on every side;
While they take counsel together against me,
They scheme to take away my life.

14 But as for me, I trust in You, O Lord;
I say, "You are my God."

15 My times are in Your hand;
Deliver me from the hand of my enemies,
And from those who persecute me.

16 Make Your face shine upon Your servant;
Save me for Your mercies' sake.

17 Do not let me be ashamed, O Lord, for I
have called upon You;
Let the wicked be ashamed;
Let them be silent in the grave.

18 Let the lying lips be put to silence,
Which speak insolent things proudly and contemptuously against the righteous.

19 Oh, how great is Your goodness,
Which You have laid up for those who fear You,
Which You have prepared for those who
trust in You
In the presence of the sons of men!

20 You shall hide them in the secret place of
Your presence
From the plots of man;
You shall keep them secretly in a pavilion
From the strife of tongues.

21 Blessed be the Lord, For He has shown me His marvelous kindness in a strong city!

22 For I said in my haste, "I am cut off from before Your eyes";
Nevertheless You heard the voice of my
supplications
When I cried out to You.

23 Oh, love the Lord, all you His saints!

For the Lord preserves the faithful,
And fully repays the proud person.

24 Be of good courage,
And He shall strengthen your heart,
All you who hope in the Lord.

PSALM 27
THE LORD IS MY LIGHT AND MY SALVATION

A Psalm of David.

1 The Lord is my light and my salvation;
Whom shall I fear?
The Lord is the strength of my life;
Of whom shall I be afraid?

2 When the wicked came against me
To eat up my flesh,
My enemies and foes,
They stumbled and fell.

3 Though an army may encamp against me,
My heart shall not fear;
Though war should rise against me,
In this I will be confident.

4 One thing I have desired of the Lord,
That will I seek:
That I may dwell in the house of the Lord
All the days of my life,
To behold the beauty of the Lord,
And to inquire in His temple.

5 For in the time of trouble
He shall hide me in His pavilion;
In the secret place of His tabernacle
He shall hide me;
He shall set me high upon a rock.

6 And now my head shall be lifted up above
my enemies all around me;
Therefore I will offer sacrifices of joy in His tabernacle;
I will sing, yes, I will sing praises to the
Lord.

7 Hear, O Lord, when I cry with my voice!
Have mercy also upon me, and answer me.

8 When You said, "Seek My face,"
My heart said to You, "Your face, Lord, I
will seek."

9 Do not hide Your face from me;

Do not turn Your servant away in anger;
You have been my help;
Do not leave me nor forsake me,
O God of my salvation.

10 When my father and my mother forsake me,
Then the Lord will take care of me.

11 Teach me Your way, O Lord, And lead me in a smooth path, because of my enemies.

12 Do not deliver me to the will of my adversaries;
For false witnesses have risen against me,
And such as breathe out violence.

13 I would have lost heart, unless I had
believed
That I would see the goodness of the Lord
In the land of the living.

14 Wait on the Lord;
Be of good courage,
And He shall strengthen your heart;
Wait, I say, on the Lord!

PSALM 40
PRAISE FOR DELIVERANCE

To the Chief Musician. A Psalm of David

1   I waited patiently for the Lord;
And He inclined to me,
And heard my cry.

2   He also brought me up out of a horrible pit,
Out of the miry clay,
And set my feet upon a rock,
And established my steps.

3   He has put a new song in my mouth--
Praise to our God;
Many will see it and fear,
And will trust in the Lord.

4   Blessed is that man who makes the Lord his trust, And does not respect the proud, nor such as turn aside to lies.

5   Many, O Lord my God, are Your
wonderful works
Which You have done;
And Your thoughts toward us
Cannot be recounted to You in order;
If I would declare and speak of them,
They are more than can be numbered.

6   Sacrifice and offering You did not desire;
My ears You have opened.
Burnt offering and sin offering You did not
require.

7   Then I said, "Behold, I come;
In the scroll of the book it is written of me.

8   I delight to do Your will, O my God,
And Your law is within my heart."

9   I have proclaimed the good news of righteousness
In the great assembly;
Indeed, I do not restrain my lips,
O Lord, You Yourself know.

10   I have not hidden Your righteousness within my heart;

I have declared Your faithfulness and Your
salvation;
I have not concealed Your lovingkindness
and Your truth
From the great assembly.

11 Do not withhold Your tender mercies from me,
O Lord;
Let Your lovingkindness and Your truth
continually preserve me.

12 For innumerable evils have surrounded me;
My iniquities have overtaken me,
so that I am not able to look up;
They are more than the hairs of my head;
Therefore my heart fails me.

13 Be pleased, O Lord, to deliver me;
O Lord, make haste to help me!

14 Let them be ashamed and brought to mutual confusion Who seek to destroy my life;
Let them be driven backward
and brought to dishonor
Who wish me evil.

15 Let them be confounded because of their shame, Who say to me, "Aha, aha!"

16 Let all those who seek You rejoice and be
glad in You;
Let such as love Your salvation say continually, "The Lord be magnified!"

17 But I am poor and needy;
Yet the Lord thinks upon me.
You are my help and my deliverer;
Do not delay, O my God.

PSALM 21
PRAISE FOR DELIVERANCE

To the Chief Musician. A Psalm of David.

1 The king shall have joy in Your strength,
O Lord;
And in Your salvation how greatly shall he rejoice!

2 You have given him his heart's desire,
And have not withheld the request of his lips.
Selah

3 For You meet him with the blessings of goodness; You set a crown of pure gold upon his head.

4 He asked life from You, and You gave it to him-- Length of days forever and ever.

5 His glory is great in Your salvation;
Honor and majesty You have placed upon him.

6 For You have made him most blessed forever;
You have made him exceedingly glad with Your presence.

7 For the king trusts in the Lord,
And through the mercy of the Most High
he shall not be moved.

8 Your hand will find all Your enemies;
Your right hand will find those who hate You.

9 You shall make them as a fiery oven in the time of Your anger;
The Lord shall swallow them up in His wrath,
And the fire shall devour them.

10 Their offspring You shall destroy from the earth,
And their descendants from among the sons of men.

11 For they intended evil against You;
They devised a plot which they are not able to perform.

12 Therefore You will make them turn their back;
You will make ready Your arrows on Your string toward their faces.

13 Be exalted, O Lord, in Your own strength!
We will sing and praise Your power.

PSALM 47
GOD IS THE KING OF ALL THE EARTH

To the Chief Musician. A Psalm of the sons of Korah.

1   Oh, clap your hands, all you peoples!
Shout to God with the voice of triumph!

2 For the Lord Most High is awesome; He is a great King over all the earth.

3 He will subdue the peoples under us,
And the nations under our feet.

4 He will choose our inheritance for us,
The excellence of Jacob whom He loves.
Selah

5 God has gone up with a shout,
The Lord with the sound of a trumpet.

6 Sing praises to God, sing praises!
Sing praises to our King, sing praises!

7 For God is the King of all the earth;
Sing praises with understanding.

8 God reigns over the nations;
God sits on His holy throne.

9 The princes of the people have gathered together, The people of the God of Abraham.
For the shields of the earth belong to God;
He is greatly exalted.

PSALM 70
A PRAYER FOR DELIVERANCE

To the Chief Musician. A Psalm of David. To bring to remembrance.

1 Make haste, O God, to deliver me!
Make haste to help me, O Lord!

2 Let them be ashamed and confounded
Who seek my life;
Let them be turned back and confused
Who desire my hurt.

3 Let them be turned back because of their shame, Who say, "Aha, aha!"

4 Let all those who seek You rejoice and be glad in You; And let those who love Your salvation say continually, "Let God be magnified!"

5 But I am poor and needy;
Make haste to me, O God!
You are my help and my deliverer;
O Lord, do not delay.

PSALM 71
GOD THE ROCK OF SALVATION

1 In You, O Lord, I put my trust;
Let me never be put to shame.

2 Deliver me in Your righteousness,
and cause me to escape;
Incline Your ear to me, and save me.

3 Be my strong refuge,
To which I may resort continually;
You have given the commandment to save me,
For You are my rock and my fortress.

4 Deliver me, O my God, out of the hand of the wicked, Out of the hand of the unrighteous and cruel man.

5 For You are my hope, O Lord God;
You are my trust from my youth.

6 By You I have been upheld from birth;
You are He who took me out of my mother's womb.
My praise shall be continually of You.

7 I have become as a wonder to many,
But You are my strong refuge.

8 Let my mouth be filled with Your praise
And with Your glory all the day.

9 Do not cast me off in the time of old age;
Do not forsake me when my strength fails.

10 For my enemies speak against me;
And those who lie in wait for my life
take counsel together,

11 Saying, "God has forsaken him;
Pursue and take him,
for there is none to deliver him."

12 O God, do not be far from me;
O my God, make haste to help me!

13 Let them be confounded and consumed
Who are adversaries of my life;

Let them be covered with reproach and dishonor
Who seek my hurt.

14 But I will hope continually,
And will praise You yet more and more.

15 My mouth shall tell of Your righteousness
And Your salvation all the day,
For I do not know their limits.

16 I will go in the strength of the Lord God;
I will make mention of Your righteousness,
of Yours only.

17 O God, You have taught me from my youth;
And to this day I declare Your wondrous works.

18 Now also when I am old and grayheaded,
O God, do not forsake me,
Until I declare Your strength to this generation,
Your power to everyone who is to come.

19 Also Your righteousness, O God, is very high,
You who have done great things;
O God, who is like You?

20 You, who have shown me great and severe troubles, Shall revive me again,
And bring me up again from the depths of the earth.

21 You shall increase my greatness,
And comfort me on every side.

22 Also with the lute I will praise you--
And Your faithfulness, O my God!
To You I will sing with the harp,
O Holy One of Israel.

23 My lips shall greatly rejoice when I sing to You,
And my soul, which You have redeemed.

24 My tongue also shall talk of Your
righteousness all the day long;
For they are confounded,
For they are brought to shame Who seek my hurt.

PSALM 107
THE LORD DELIVERS FROM TROUBLE

1 Oh, give thanks to the Lord, for He is good!
For His mercy endures forever.

2 Let the redeemed of the Lord say so,
Whom He has redeemed from the hand of the enemy,

3 And gathered out of the lands,
From the east and from the west,
From the north and from the south.

4 They wandered in the wilderness in a desolate way; They found no city to dwell in.

5 Hungry and thirsty,
Their soul fainted in them.

6 Then they cried out to the Lord in their trouble,
And He delivered them out of their distresses.

7 And He led them forth by the right way,
That they might go to a city for a dwelling place.

8 Oh, that men would give thanks to
the Lord for His goodness,
And for His wonderful works to the children of men!

9 For He satisfies the longing soul,
And fills the hungry soul with goodness.

10 Those who sat in darkness and in
the shadow of death,
Bound in affliction and irons--

11 Because they rebelled against the words of God, And despised the counsel of the Most High,

12 Therefore He brought down their heart with labor; They fell down, and there was none to help.

13 Then they cried out to the Lord in their trouble,
And He saved them out of their distresses.

14 He brought them out of darkness and
the shadow of death,
And broke their chains in pieces.

15 Oh, that men would give thanks to
the Lord for His goodness,
And for His wonderful works to the children of men!

16 For He has broken the gates of bronze, And cut the bars of iron in two.

17 Fools, because of their transgression,
And because of their iniquities, were afflicted.

18 Their soul abhorred all manner of food, And they drew near to the gates of death.

19 Then they cried out to the Lord in their trouble,
And He saved them out of their distresses.

20 He sent His word and healed them, And delivered them from their destructions.

21 Oh, that men would give thanks to
the Lord for His goodness,
And for His wonderful works to the children of men!

22 Let them sacrifice the sacrifices of thanksgiving,
And declare His works with rejoicing.

23 Those who go down to the sea in ships,
Who do business on great waters,

24 They see the works of the Lord,
And His wonders in the deep.

25 For He commands and
raises the stormy wind,
Which lifts up the waves of the sea.

26 They mount up to the heavens,
They go down again to the depths;
Their soul melts because of trouble.

27 They reel to and fro, and stagger like
a drunken man,
And are at their wits' end.

28 Then they cry out to the Lord in their trouble,
And He brings them out of their distresses.

29 He calms the storm,
So that its waves are still.

30 Then they are glad because they are quiet;
So He guides them to their desired haven.

31 Oh, that men would give thanks to
the Lord for His goodness,

And for His wonderful works to the children of men!

32 Let them exalt Him also in the assembly of
the people,
And praise Him in the company of the elders.

33 He turns rivers into a wilderness,
And the watersprings into dry ground;

34 A fruitful land into barrenness,
For the wickedness of those who dwell in it.

35 He turns a wilderness into pools of water, And dry land into watersprings.

36 There He makes the hungry dwell,
That they may establish a city for a dwelling place,

37 And sow fields and plant vineyards,
That they may yield a fruitful harvest.

38 He also blesses them,
and they multiply greatly;
And He does not let their cattle decrease.

39 When they are diminished and brought low
Through oppression, affliction and sorrow,

40 He pours contempt on princes,
And causes them to wander in the wilderness where there is no way;

41 Yet He sets the poor on high, far from affliction,
And makes their families like a flock.

42 The righteous see it and rejoice,
And all iniquity stops its mouth.

43 Whoever is wise will observe these things,
And they will understand the lovingkindness of the Lord.

PSALM 119
THE EXCELLENCE OF GOD'S LAW

1 Blessed are the undefiled in the way,
Who walk in the law of the Lord!

2 Blessed are those who keep
His testimonies,
Who seek Him with the whole heart!

3 They also do no iniquity;
They walk in His ways.

4 You have commanded us
To keep Your precepts diligently.

5 Oh, that my ways were directed
To keep Your statutes!

6 Then I would not be ashamed,
When I look into all Your commandments.

7 I will praise You with uprightness of heart,
When I learn Your righteous judgments.

8 I will keep Your statutes;
Oh, do not forsake me utterly!

9 How can a young man cleanse his way?
By taking heed according to Your word.

10 With my whole heart I have sought You;
Oh, let me not wander from Your commandments!

11 Your word I have hidden in my heart,
that I might not sin against You!

12 Blessed are You, O Lord!
Teach me Your statutes!

13 With my lips I have declared
All the judgments of Your mouth.

14 I have rejoiced in the way of Your testimonies,
As much as in all riches.

15 I will meditate on Your precepts,

And contemplate Your ways.

16 I will delight myself in Your statutes;
I will not forget Your word.

17 Deal bountifully with Your servant,
That I may live and keep Your word.

18 Open my eyes,
that I may see Wondrous things from Your law.

19 I am a stranger in the earth;
Do not hide Your commandments from me.

20 My soul breaks with longing
For Your judgments at all times.

21 You rebuke the proud--the cursed,
Who stray from Your commandments.

22 Remove from me reproach and contempt,
For I have kept Your testimonies.

23 Princes also sit and speak against me, But Your servant meditates on Your statutes.

24 Your testimonies also are my delight
And my counselors.

25 My soul clings to the dust;
Revive me according to Your word.

26 I have declared my ways, and You answered me; Teach me Your statutes.

27 Make me understand the way of Your precepts;
So shall I meditate on Your wondrous works.

28 My soul melts from heaviness;
Strengthen me according to Your word.

29 Remove from me the way of lying, And grant me Your law graciously.

30 I have chosen the way of truth;
Your judgments I have laid before me.

31 I cling to Your testimonies;
O Lord, do not put me to shame!

32 I will run the course of Your commandments,
For You shall enlarge my heart.

33 Teach me, O Lord,
the way of Your statutes,
And I shall keep it to the end.

34 Give me understanding, and
I shall keep Your law;
Indeed, I shall observe it with my whole heart.

35 Make me walk in the path of
Your commandments,
For I delight in it.

36 Incline my heart to Your testimonies,
And not to covetousness.

37 Turn away my eyes from looking at
worthless things,
And revive me in Your way.

38 Establish Your word to Your servant,
Who is devoted to fearing You.

39 Turn away my reproach which I dread,
For Your judgments are good.

40 Behold, I long for Your precepts;
Revive me in Your righteousness.

41 Let Your mercies come also to me, O Lord--
Your salvation according to Your word.

42 So shall I have an answer for him who
reproaches me,
For I trust in Your word.

43 And take not the word of truth utterly out
of my mouth,
For I have hoped in Your ordinances.

44 So shall I keep Your law continually,
Forever and ever.

45 And I will walk at liberty,
For I seek Your precepts.

46 I will speak of Your testimonies also before kings, And will not be ashamed.

47 And I will delight myself in Your commandments, Which I love.

48 My hands also I will lift up to
Your commandments, Which I love,
And I will meditate on Your statutes.

49 Remember the word to Your servant,
Upon which You have caused me to hope.

50 This is my comfort in my affliction,
For Your word has given me life.

51 The proud have me in great derision,
Yet I do not turn aside from Your law.

52 I remembered Your judgments of old,
O Lord, And have comforted myself.

53 Indignation has taken hold of me Because of the wicked, who forsake Your law.

54 Your statutes have been my songs In the house of my pilgrimage.

55 I remember Your name in the night,
O Lord, And I keep Your law.

56 This has become mine,
Because I kept Your precepts.

57 You are my portion, O Lord;
I have said that I would keep Your words.

58 I entreated Your favor with my whole heart;
Be merciful to me according to Your word.

59 I thought about my ways,
And turned my feet to Your testimonies.

60 I made haste, and did not delay
To keep Your commandments.

61 The cords of the wicked have bound me,
But I have not forgotten Your law.

62 At midnight I will rise to give thanks to You, Because of Your righteous judgments.

63 I am a companion of all who fear You,
And of those who keep Your precepts.

64 The earth, O Lord, is full of Your mercy;
Teach me Your statutes.

65 You have dealt well with Your servant,
O Lord, according to Your word.

66 Teach me good judgment and knowledge,
For I believe Your commandments.

67 Before I was afflicted I went astray,
But now I keep Your word.

68 You are good, and do good;
Teach me Your statutes.

69 The proud have forged a lie against me,
But I will keep Your precepts with my whole heart.

70 Their heart is as fat as grease,
But I delight in Your law.

71 It is good for me that I have been afflicted,
That I may learn Your statutes.

72 The law of Your mouth is better to me
Than thousands of coins of gold and silver.

73 Your hands have made me and fashioned me; Give me understanding, that I may learn Your commandments.

74 Those who fear You will be glad when
they see me,
Because I have hoped in Your word.

75 I know, O Lord, that Your judgments are right,
And that in faithfulness You have afflicted me.

76 Let, I pray, Your merciful kindness be for
my comfort,
According to Your word to Your servant.

77 Let Your tender mercies come to me,
that I may live;
For Your law is my delight.

78 Let the proud be ashamed,
For they treated me wrongfully with falsehood;
But I will meditate on Your precepts.

79 Let those who fear You turn to me,
Those who know Your testimonies.

80 Let my heart be blameless regarding
Your statutes,
That I may not be ashamed.

81 My soul faints for Your salvation,
But I hope in Your word.

82 My eyes fail from searching Your word,
Saying, "When will You comfort me?"

83 For I have become like a wineskin in smoke,
Yet I do not forget Your statutes.

84 How many are the days of Your servant?
When will You execute judgment on
those who persecute me?

85 The proud have dug pits for me,
Which is not according to Your law.

86 All Your commandments are faithful;
They persecute me wrongfully;
Help me!

87 They almost made an end of me on earth,
But I did not forsake Your precepts.

88 Revive me according to Your lovingkindness,
So that I may keep the testimony of Your mouth.

89 Forever, O Lord, Your word is settled in heaven.

90 Your faithfulness endures to all generations;
You established the earth, and it abides.

91 They continue this day according to
Your ordinances,
For all are Your servants.

92 Unless Your law had been my delight,
I would then have perished in my affliction.

93 I will never forget Your precepts,
For by them You have given me life.

94 I am Yours, save me;
For I have sought Your precepts.

95 The wicked wait for me to destroy me,
But I will consider Your testimonies.

96 I have seen the consummation of all perfection, But Your commandment is exceedingly broad.

97 Oh, how I love Your law!
It is my meditation all the day.

98 You, through Your commandments, make me wiser than my enemies;
For they are ever with me.

99 I have more understanding than all my teachers,
For Your testimonies are my meditation.

100 I understand more than the ancients,
Because I keep Your precepts.

101 I have restrained my feet from every evil way, That I may keep Your word.

102 I have not departed from Your judgments,
For You Yourself have taught me.

103 How sweet are Your words to my taste,
Sweeter than honey to my mouth!

104 Through Your precepts I get understanding; Therefore I hate every false way.

105 Your word is a lamp to my feet
And a light to my path.

106 I have sworn and confirmed
That I will keep Your righteous judgments.

107 I am afflicted very much;
Revive me, O Lord, according to Your word.

108 Accept, I pray, the freewill offerings of my mouth, O Lord, And teach me Your judgments.

109 My life is continually in my hand, Yet I do not forget Your law.

110 The wicked have laid a snare for me,
Yet I have not strayed from Your precepts.

111 Your testimonies I have taken as
a heritage forever,
For they are the rejoicing of my heart.

112 I have inclined my heart to perform Your statutes Forever, to the very end.

113 I hate the double-minded,
But I love Your law.

114 You are my hiding place and my shield;
I hope in Your word.

115 Depart from me, you evildoers,
For I will keep the commandments of my God!

116 Uphold me according to Your word,
that I may live;
And do not let me be ashamed of my hope.

117 Hold me up, and I shall be safe,
And I shall observe Your statutes continually.

118 You reject all those who stray from
Your statutes, For their deceit is falsehood.

119 You put away all the wicked of the earth like dross; Therefore I love Your testimonies.

120 My flesh trembles for fear of You,
And I am afraid of Your judgments.

121 I have done justice and righteousness;
Do not leave me to my oppressors.

122 Be surety for Your servant for good;
Do not let the proud oppress me.

123 My eyes fail from seeking Your salvation And Your righteous word.

124 Deal with Your servant according to Your mercy, And teach me Your statutes.

125 I am Your servant; Give me understanding,
That I may know Your testimonies.

126 It is time for You to act, O Lord,
For they have regarded Your law as void.

127 Therefore I love Your commandments
More than gold, yes, than fine gold!

128 Therefore all Your precepts concerning
all things I consider to be right;
I hate every false way.

129 Your testimonies are wonderful;
Therefore my soul keeps them.

130 The entrance of Your words gives light;
It gives understanding to the simple.

131 I opened my mouth and panted,
For I longed for Your commandments.

132 Look upon me and be merciful to me,
As Your custom is toward those who love Your name.

133 Direct my steps by Your word, And let no iniquity have dominion over me.

134 Redeem me from the oppression of man,
That I may keep Your precepts.

135 Make Your face shine upon Your servant,
And teach me Your statutes.

136 Rivers of water run down from my eyes, Because men do not keep Your law.

137 Righteous are You, O Lord,
And upright are Your judgments.

138 Your testimonies, which You have commanded,
Are righteous and very faithful.

139 My zeal has consumed me,
Because my enemies have forgotten Your words.

140 Your word is very pure;
Therefore Your servant loves it.

141 I am small and despised,
Yet I do not forget Your precepts.

142 Your righteousness is
an everlasting righteousness,
And Your law is truth.

143 Trouble and anguish have overtaken me,
Yet Your commandments are my delights.

144 The righteousness of Your testimonies is everlasting;
Give me understanding, and I shall live.

145 I cry out with my whole heart;
Hear me, O Lord! I will keep Your statutes.

146 I cry out to You; Save me, and I will keep Your testimonies.

147 I rise before the dawning of the morning,
And cry for help; I hope in Your word.

148 My eyes are awake through the night watches, That I may meditate on Your word.

149 Hear my voice according to Your lovingkindness; O Lord, revive me according to Your justice.

150 They draw near who follow after wickedness; They are far from Your law.

151 You are near, O Lord,
And all Your commandments are truth.

152 Concerning Your testimonies,
I have known of old that
You have founded them forever.

153 Consider my affliction and deliver me,
For I do not forget Your law.

154 Plead my cause and redeem me;
Revive me according to Your word.

155 Salvation is far from the wicked,
For they do not seek Your statutes.

156 Great are Your tender mercies, O Lord;
Revive me according to Your judgments.

157 Many are my persecutors and my enemies,
Yet I do not turn from Your testimonies.

158 I see the treacherous, and am disgusted, Because they do not keep Your word.

159 Consider how I love Your precepts;
Revive me, O Lord, according to Your lovingkindness.

160 The entirety of Your word is truth,
And every one of Your righteous judgments endures forever.

161 Princes persecute me without a cause,
But my heart stands in awe of Your word.

162 I rejoice at Your word
As one who finds great treasure.

163 I hate and abhor lying,
But I love Your law.

164 Seven times a day I praise You,
Because of Your righteous judgments.

165 Great peace have those who love Your law,
And nothing causes them to stumble.

166 Lord, I hope for Your salvation,
And I do Your commandments.

167 My soul keeps Your testimonies,
And I love them exceedingly.

168 I keep Your precepts and Your testimonies,
For all my ways are before You.

169 Let my cry come before You, O Lord;
Give me understanding according to Your word.

170 Let my supplication come before You;
Deliver me according to Your word.

171 My lips shall utter praise,
For You teach me Your statutes.

172 My tongue shall speak of Your word,
For all Your commandments are righteousness.

173 Let Your hand become my help,
For I have chosen Your precepts.

174 I long for Your salvation, O Lord,
And Your law is my delight.

175 Let my soul live, and it shall praise You;
And let Your judgments help me.

176 I have gone astray like a lost sheep;
Seek Your servant,
For I do not forget Your commandments.

PSALM 120
A PRAYER FOR DELIVERANCE FROM DECEITFULNESS

A Song of Ascents.

1 In my distress I cried to the Lord,
And He heard me.

2 Deliver my soul, O Lord, from lying lips
And from a deceitful tongue.

3 What shall be given to you,
Or what shall be done to you,
You false tongue?

4 Sharp arrows of the warrior,
With coals of the broom tree!

5 Woe is me, that I dwell in Meshech,
That I dwell among the tents of Kedar!

6 My soul has dwelt too long
With one who hates peace.

7 I am for peace;
But when I speak, they are for war.

PSALM 148
PRAISE TO THE LORD FROM CREATION

1 Praise the Lord! Praise the Lord from the heavens; Praise Him in the heights!

2 Praise Him, all His angels;
Praise Him, all His hosts!

3 Praise Him, sun and moon;
Praise Him, all you stars of light!

4 Praise Him, you heavens of heavens,
And you waters above the heavens!

5 Let them praise the name of the Lord,
For He commanded and they were created.

6 He also established them forever and ever;
He made a decree which shall not pass away.

7 Praise the Lord from the earth,
You great sea creatures and all the depths;

8 Fire and hail, snow and clouds;
Stormy wind, fulfilling His word;

9 Mountains and all hills;
Fruitful trees and all cedars;

10 Beasts and all cattle;
Creeping things and flying fowl;

11 Kings of the earth and all peoples;
Princes and all judges of the earth;

12 Both young men and maidens;
Old men and children.

13 Let them praise the name of the Lord,
For His name alone is exalted;
His glory is above the earth and heaven.

14 And He has exalted the horn of His people,
The praise of all His saints--
Of the children of Israel,
A people near to Him.

Praise the Lord!

PSALM 149
PRAISE THE LORD FOR HIS SALVATION AND JUDGEMENT

1 Praise the Lord! Sing to the Lord a new song,
And His praise in the assembly of saints.

2 Let Israel rejoice in their Maker;
Let the children of Zion be joyful in their King.

3 Let them praise His name with the dance;
Let them sing praises to Him with the timbrel and harp.

4 For the Lord takes pleasure in His people;
He will beautify the humble with salvation.

5 Let the saints be joyful in glory;
Let them sing aloud on their beds.

6 Let the high praises of God be in their mouth,
And a two-edged sword in their hand,

7 To execute vengeance on the nations,
And punishments on the peoples;

8 To bind their kings with chains,
And their nobles with fetters of iron;

9 To execute on them the written judgment--
This honor have all His saints.

Praise the Lord!

PSALM 66
PRAISE FOR GOD'S MIGHTY DEEDS

To the Chief Musician. A Song. A Psalm.

1 Make a joyful shout to God, all the earth!

2 Sing out the honor of His name;
Make His praise glorious.

3 Say to God, "How awesome are Your works!
Through the greatness of Your power
Your enemies shall submit themselves to You.

4 All the earth shall worship You
And sing praises to You;
They shall sing praises to Your name."
Selah

5 Come and see the works of God;
He is awesome in His doing toward the sons of men.

6 He turned the sea into dry land;
They went through the river on foot.
There we will rejoice in Him.

7 He rules by His power forever;
His eyes observe the nations;
Do not let the rebellious exalt themselves.
Selah

8 Oh, bless our God, you peoples!
And make the voice of His praise to be heard,

9 Who keeps our soul among the living,
And does not allow our feet to be moved.

10 For You, O God, have tested us;
You have refined us as silver is refined.

11 You brought us into the net;
You laid affliction on our backs.

12 You have caused men to ride over our heads;
We went through fire and through water;
But You brought us out to rich fulfillment.

13 I will go into Your house with burnt offerings;

I will pay You my vows,

14 Which my lips have uttered
And my mouth has spoken when I was in trouble.

15 I will offer You burnt sacrifices of fat animals,
With the sweet aroma of rams;
I will offer bulls with goats.
Selah

16 Come and hear, all you who fear God,
And I will declare what He has done for my soul.

17 I cried to Him with my mouth,
And He was extolled with my tongue.

18 If I regard iniquity in my heart,
The Lord will not hear.

19 But certainly God has heard me;
He has attended to the voice of my prayer.

20 Blessed be God,
Who has not turned away my prayer,
Nor His mercy from me!

PSALM 76
THE GOD OF VICTORY AND JUDGEMENT

To the Chief Musician. On stringed instruments.
A Psalm of Asaph. A Song.

1 In Judah God is known;
His name is great in Israel.

2 In Salem also is His tabernacle,
And His dwelling place in Zion.

3 There He broke the arrows of the bow,
The shield and sword of battle.
Selah

4 You are more glorious and excellent
Than the mountains of prey.

5 The stouthearted were plundered;
They have sunk into their sleep;
And none of the mighty men have found the use of their hands.

6 At Your rebuke, O God of Jacob,
Both the chariot and horse were cast into a dead sleep.

7 You, Yourself, are to be feared;
And who may stand in Your presence
When once You are angry?

8 You caused judgment to be heard from heaven;
The earth feared and was still,

9 When God arose to judgment,
To deliver all the oppressed of the earth.
Selah

10 Surely the wrath of man shall praise You;
With the remainder of wrath
You shall gird Yourself.

11 Make vows to the Lord your God, and pay them;
Let all who are around Him bring presents to
Him who ought to be feared.

12 He shall cut off the spirit of princes;
He is awesome to the kings of the earth.

CHAPTER 17

MY LETTER TO PARENTS:

EDUCATE YOUR CHILDREN

Dear parents,

As a parent, have you ever imagined why God gave you your children? Do you know that there are people looking for children for many years and have not been blessed with the fruit of the womb?

"Behold, children are a heritage from the Lord , The fruit of the womb is a reward. Like arrows in the hand of a warrior, So are the children of one's youth. Happy is the man who has his quiver full of them; They shall not be ashamed, But shall speak with their enemies in the gate." (Psalm 127:3-5.)

Do you know that children come from the Lord and He gave you your children so that you can take proper care of them? Do you know that the Lord will not be happy with you if He blessed you with children and you failed to take proper care of them?

"And you, fathers, do not provoke your children to wrath, but bring them up in the training and admonition of the Lord." (Ephesians 6:4)

If you are a parent or guardian, please take good care of your children or those entrusted unto your care, for there are enormous blessings from the Lord when you do so. Even if they are not your own children, as long as they are in your care, please take care of them and do it for the Lord who will reward you accordingly.

"Train up a child in the way he should go, And when he is old he will not depart from it." (Proverbs 22:6)

As a parent, don't fail to take care of your children and educate them no matter the circumstances you find yourself. You must learn to sacrifice a lot of things so that you can be able to educate your children properly. You must learn to do away with certain unnecessary pleasures so that you can take proper care of your children and send them to school.

"Take heed that you do not despise one of these little ones, for I say to you that in heaven their angels always see the face of My Father who is in heaven."
(Matthew 18:10)

If as a parent your own parents did not send you to school when you were young, don't transfer such grudge unto your own children and refuse to send them to school just because your own parents could not educate you during your own time. Times have changed and things have changed. We are no longer in the olden days, so don't allow the mistakes of your own parents to affect your own children. They have done their own and probably gone to join their ancestors, so discharge your own responsibilities to your own children.

If every child born on the surface of this earth is properly trained and educated with good moral values and etiquette, the violence, hatred and moral decadence in our society today will be greatly reduced to the barest minimum. If every child is well trained to inculcate good moral values, the society will be far better off and safer for all of us to live in.

As a parent, if you know you cannot take care of your children, please don't bring them into this world to suffer. If you know you are not capable, don't exert yourself above your capabilities. Many people are suffering today because of the failure of their parents to train them or send them to school even when those parents had the money but they ignorantly, knowingly or unknowingly refused to send their children to school or to plan for the future of those children.

The family unit is the smallest unit in any society and it is the root of the society because whatever affects the family will ultimately affect the larger society. If the family is stable and morally sound, it will eventually rub off on the larger society because there can never be a society in the first place without the family.

As a parent, your priority in life should be to take care of your children properly, to inculcate good moral values into them, to train them in the way of the Lord and to send them to the best schools or anyone you can afford. You must realize that it's a commandment from the Lord that parents must take care of their children.

"But if anyone does not provide for his own, and especially for those of his household, he has denied the faith and is worse than an unbeliever." (1st Timothy 5:8)

If the Lord has blessed you with children and you refused to take care of them despite you have the means to do so, the Lord will not be happy with you and this can even block a lot of blessings and close a lot of doors for you.

"At that time the disciples came to Jesus, saying, 'Who then is greatest in the kingdom of heaven?' Then Jesus called a little child to Him, set him in the midst of them, and said, 'Assuredly, I say to you, unless you are converted and become as little children, you will by no means enter the kingdom of heaven. Therefore whoever humbles himself as this little child is the greatest in the kingdom of heaven. Whoever receives one little child like this in My name receives Me. Whoever causes one of these little ones who believe in Me to sin, it would be better for him if a millstone were hung around his neck, and he were drowned in the depth of the sea.'" (Matthew 18:1-6)

As a parent, you must realize that education is the best legacy you can give to your children. You can leave behind hectares of land, landed properties and houses or mansions for your children; yes this is good and commendable, but education is the best legacy and the best investment you can give to your children.

When you give them education and training to acquire valuable skills, you have automatically taught them how to catch the fish that will feed them for the rest of their lives, instead of giving them fish by yourself. A child without proper upbringing and education can squander or mismanage the properties left behind by their parents, but the one with sound training, both morally, spiritually and academically will not do so.

So no matter the circumstances, as a parent, strive hard to educate your children. It's not always rosy for everybody at all times. There will surely be challenges along the line but you must never give up. You must invest in the future of your children and when they grow up, things will become easier because of the foundation you've laid for them. And by then you will see that you'll even have peace and rest of mind knowing that your children are in the best positions.

As you do this, may the Lord bless you abundantly. May He send you help from the Sanctuary. The Lord will bless you and multiply your finances in Jesus name. Amen. As you do this, the Lord will open new doors of grace, mercy and favor for you in Jesus name. Those children will grow up and become good citizens and become useful to your family and to the society at large.

The peace of the Lord be with you in Jesus name. Amen.

Yours Sincerely,

Tayo Demola

Lagos, Nigeria

December 23, 2019.

CONSULTATION, COUNSELING AND PRAYERS

Is there any area of your life you need the Lord to visit you and do a miracle in your life?

Is it in your business, life, relationship, marriage, health, family, finances or any other area of life?

Are you sick with any kind of ailment or disease?

Do you need supernatural healing for any ailment or disease?

Do you believe that our Lord Jesus Christ can do it for you?

The Lord Jesus Christ will touch your life positively and bless you. Amen.

For consultation, counseling and prayers, Whatsapp Prophet Tayo on +2348038029980 or send a mail to prophettayo447@gmail.com

God bless you.

PARTNER WITH ME

Have you been blessed by this book?

Would you like to partner with me to spread the gospel of our Lord Jesus Christ round the world?

Would you like to support our work of healing the sick, delivering the oppressed and setting the captives free?

Would you like to donate and sow a seed into my ministry to support the work of God?

If so, then send me a mail via prophettayo447@gmail.com or chat me on Whatsapp +2348038029980.

As you do so, may the good Lord bless and multiply you abundantly in Jesus name. Amen.

KINDLY DROP A REVIEW

Have you enjoyed reading this book? Have you been blessed by the content of this book?

Kindly drop a review of this book on your favorite online store and let's know what you think about the book.

God bless you as you do so in Jesus name. Amen.

ABOUT THE AUTHOR

Prophet Tayo Demola is a man of many parts; a multi talented Nigerian and a beacon of hope to millions of people, having inspired many via his books, teachings and writings.

He is a Prophet of the Most High God, Healing Evangelist, Pastor, Human Rights Activist, Relationship Coach, Editor, Publisher, Singer, Songwriter, Gospel Artist & Entrepreneur. He has motivated and impacted the lives of millions of Nigerians from various walks of life through his powerful motivational messages and writings.

He has authored several books, some of which are Passions of Love, Success Golden Principles, Motivations For Success, 30 Habits That Destroy Relationships, among others.

He is a Prophet and Minister of the gospel of our Lord Jesus Christ, filled with the Holy Spirit and with the gift of tongues among several other spiritual gifts.

He was called by our Lord Jesus Christ as a prophet and servant of the Most High God to the nations for the spiritual emancipation of the people and salvation of mankind.

www.ingramcontent.com/pod-product-compliance
Lightning Source LLC
Chambersburg PA
CBHW071512220526
45472CB00003B/995